The International Society for Science & Religion was established in 2002 to promote education through the support of inter-disciplinary learning and research in the fields of science and religion. Our current membership of 140 comes from all major faith traditions and includes non-religious scholars. Inducted by nomination only, they are drawn from leading research institutions and academies worldwide. The Society embraces all perspectives that are supported by excellent scholarship.

In 2007, the Society began the process of creating a unique resource, *The ISSR Library*, a comprehensive reference and teaching tool for scholars, students, and interested lay readers. This collection spans the essential ideas and arguments that frame studies in science, religion, and the human spirit.

The Library has been selected through a rigorous process of peer review. Each constituent volume makes a substantial contribution to the field or stands as an important referent. These books exhibit the highest quality of scholarship and present distinct, influential viewpoints, some of which are controversial. While the many perspectives in these volumes are not individually endorsed by the ISSR, each reflects a facet of the field that is worthy of attention.

Accompanying the Library is *The ISSR Companion to Science and Religion*, a volume containing brief introductory essays on each of the Library's constituents. Users are encouraged to refer to the *Companion* or our website for an overview of the Library.

For a complete list of Contributing Editors, please visit
www.issrlibrary.org/contributingeditors

For a complete list of Library Selections please visit
www.issrlibrary.org/selections

A
FEMINIST
COSMOLOGY

A
FEMINIST
COSMOLOGY

ecology, solidarity,
and
metaphysics

NANCY R. HOWELL

Humanity
Books

an imprint of Prometheus Books
59 John Glenn Drive, Amherst, New York 14228-2197

Published 2000 by Humanity Books, an imprint of Prometheus Books

Inquiries should be addressed to
Humanity Books
59 John Glenn Drive
Amherst, New York 14228–2197
VOICE: 716–691–0133, ext. 207
FAX: 716–564–2711

04 03 02 01 00   5 4 3 2 1

Library of Congress Cataloging-in-Publication Data

Howell, Nancy R., 1953–
    A feminist cosmology : ecology, solidarity, and metaphysics / Nancy R. Howell.
      p. cm.
    Based on the author's thesis—Claremont Graduate School.
    Includes bibliographical references (p.) and index.
    ISBN 1–57392–653–1 (alk. paper)
    1. Feminist theory. 2. Ecofeminism. 3. Cosmology. 4. Metaphysics. 5. Process
philosophy. I. Title.

HQ1190.H68 2000
305.42—dc21
                                                        97–13529
                                                           CIP

Printed in the United States of America on acid-free paper

CONTENTS

ACKNOWLEDGMENTS

MY REFLECTION ON A Whiteheadian feminist cosmology based on Whitehead's relational epistemology was itself undertaken in a relational context that has been both instructive and supportive. I am grateful to John B. Cobb Jr., who encouraged me to be creative, rigorous, and precise, and to others who served as members of my dissertation committee, June O'Connor, Dan Rhoades, John Hick, and Jack Verheyden. The current manuscript has matured considerably since the dissertation, but stands on the shoulders of good advice from my mentors and friends at Claremont Graduate School. I am indebted to numerous peers and colleagues at the Claremont Graduate School, especially "Tess" Tessier and Dagfinn Aslid, for conversations that stimulated this work. This project was shaped significantly by the resources and conferences of the Center for Process Studies. I am especially grateful to the Center for support from Stephen Meadors and Kathlyn A. Breazeale during the early stages of writing and to the journal *Process Studies* for publishing early drafts of chapters 2 and 4 as "The Promise of a Process Feminist Theory of Relations" (17:2) and "Radical Relatedness and Feminist Separatism" (18:2). I value an invitation from the Society of Christian Philosophers to present "A Feminist Critique of Divine Omnipotence," an early draft of portions of chapter 5, at the 1988 meeting of the Central Division of the American Philosophical Association. In recent revisions that diverge significantly from the dissertation, I am indebted to colleagues in the Department of Religion at Pacific Lutheran University who have listened patiently and read repeatedly drafts that have struggled to find just the right words. I am grateful to the Board of Regents at Pacific Lutheran University who provided a Regency Advancement Award that supported and encouraged final editing and revisions. My deepest appreciation extends to friends who had confidence in me and who were my companions while I was writing, particularly David K. Firman whose relationships with family, neighbors, animals, and with me deepened my understanding of relationships.

MAKING SENSE OF RELATIONSHIPS

MY FIRST TASTE OF feminism aroused in me a rebellion against being dependent on relationships for my identity and survival. Feminism, in my mind, was equated with learning to be self-sufficient, competitive, and independent. I adopted the "self-made man" as my role model and attempted to achieve equality by emulating a masculine norm. A nonrelational model, however, proved to be a frustrating and disappointing choice, because it ignored both the satisfaction gained from enjoying relationships and the necessity of negotiating a vast network of relationships in a complex world. My shallow and mistaken impression of feminism has been corrected by the knowledge that healthy selfhood entails independence *and* interdependence. Relationships are not merely incidental, aesthetic, or bothersome—relationships are central to the emergence of feminist selfhood.

Redirecting my thinking and living toward a consciously relational worldview and practice placed me at odds with my culture. Government and politics value individual rights. Economics favors competition among individuals. Education assesses individual achievement. Even my Protestant Christianity calls for a personal commitment. Against the tide of individualism, feminism and my own intuitions moved me to a relational stance for which I was unprepared.

Reordering my life and reconstructing my perspective in a feminist relational direction gathered energy from women's scholarship and writing. Feminist psychology has been one resource and influence. In *The Reproduction of Mothering*, Nancy Chodorow agrees with object-relations theorists that the psychological development and personality formation of a child is determined from infancy by the child's relational experience—in particular, the relational connection to the child's primary caregiver, the mother.[1] Chodorow argues from an interpretation of preoedipal development that the relationship to the mother differs for boys and girls and creates different relational capacities for boys and girls.[2] The mother-daughter relationship is the source of the capacity to mother, cyclically reproducing the capacity to mother.[3] Not only does Chodorow argue the significance of relationships in the psychological formation of persons, but she further argues that boys' and girls'

1

early relationships shape them for differing adult gender roles that identify women with reproduction and mothering in the context of a gender-unequal society.[4] Mothering, in sum, reproduces itself *and* male dominance such that family structure is a defining influence on gender and society. Dual parenting, reshaping family relationships, then has the potential to transform unequal gender relations in society.

Carol Gilligan's *In a Different Voice* furthers the discussion of women and relationships. Gilligan argues that it is inappropriate to compare women's moral development with a male norm (Kolberg's six stages of moral development), because women's greater interdependence and relational orientation creates in women a different process of moral development.[5] Although male moral understanding and judgment are more individualistic and focus on universal principles and individual rights, women's moral understanding and judgment are relational. Women's moral development is oriented toward preserving relationships, expressing compassion, and addressing real predicaments.[6] Gilligan argues that the relational moral capacities of women are practiced in an ethic of responsibility and care.[7]

Jean Baker Miller and researchers associated with the Stone Center are committed to a model of the "self-in-relation." Miller's *Toward a New Psychology of Women* analyzes relationships of inequality in terms of dominance and subordination. Although there are relationships of temporary inequality (such as teacher-student relationships), relations of permanent inequality are based on race, sex, class, nationality, religion, and other inborn characteristics.[8] Miller's focus is the permanent inequality in male-female relationships. Seeking the valuable characteristics of the subordinate group, Miller's "new psychology of women" assesses strengths rather than weakness in women's tendency toward affiliations. Miller argues that men are forced to center upon self and women are forced to center upon others, yet the suffering that is created by these limiting foci is unnecessary, because humans need both self and others.[9] Women's psychological development proceeds by attachment and affiliation, but for all humans, affiliation is important for development.[10] Miller's significant conclusion is that relationship creates more authentic selfhood.[11]

Women's Growth in Connection, the product of Stone Center research, more recently interprets the self-in-relation model in a collection of essays. In this volume, Jean Baker Miller defines "being-in-relationship" as the "sense of one's self as a person who attends to and responds to what is going on in the relationships between two or more people."[12] Three features of women's relationships are notable themes of the essays that follow Miller's essay. The first is empathy. Essays by Judith V. Jordan, Janet L. Surrey, and Alexandra G. Kaplan identify empathy as a complex, advanced, interactive process.[13] Jordan sees the beginning of empathy in mother-daughter relationships, supported by Kaplan's argument that the separation-individuation model should be replaced with a relationship-differentiation model.[14] The second is mutuality. In other essays by Surrey and Jordan, mutuality is named as a characteristic of intersubjective relationships that entail both affecting and responding.[15] The third is empowerment. Irene P. Stiver contends that dependency in relationships means experiencing oneself as enhanced and empowered through relying on others for help.[16] Surrey describes psychological empowerment as a creative process, energizing and motivating both participants in a relationship—empowerment is not control of one person by another in a relationship.[17]

A growing body of literature on female friendship has impacted feminist theory and has most surely stimulated my consideration of relationships. I am particularly appreciative of lesbian feminist philosophers and thealogians/ theologians. Janice G. Raymond's *A Passion for Friends* discusses Gyn/ affection as both personal and political movement of women toward each other.[18] Raymond's text urges female friendship to realize its social and political power where it is afforded no status and where male-female relationships are normative. The genealogical method supporting Raymond's philosophy discovers precedents for empowering female friendships in the hetaerocracy of the convent and in the economic and social power of Chinese marriage resisters. It is noteworthy that Raymond advocates the "worldliness" of female friendship and the impact of Gyn/affection beyond the private sphere.

Mary E. Hunt's book *Fierce Tenderness: A Feminist Theology of Friendship* picks up a similar theme and understands friendship as personal relationship *and* political activity.[19] Hunt defines friendship as "voluntary human relationships that are entered into by people who intend one another's wellbeing and who intend that their love relationship is part of a justice-seeking community."[20] Hunt describes a model for right relation, named fierce tenderness, that is characterized by love, power, embodiment, and spirituality and that applies to friendships within families, among neighbors, as couples, and in communities.[21] The fruits of female friendship are social change, an ethic rooted in women's experience, and justice-seeking coalitions.

Hunt claims that women's friendship inspires and enlarges what we can know about women, each other, the natural order, and the divine, but although Hunt does not fully pursue each of these implications, Mary Daly, in an earlier book titled *Pure Lust*, set sisterhood ontologically within a comprehensive vision of the world and women's spirituality. Be-Friending (discussed more carefully in chapter 4) is the context of female friendship. Be-Friending affirms not only female connection in its personal and activist dimensions, but the interconnection of all be-ing. "Biophilic bonding" describes the life-giving connection of women to other women, to self, and "with the sun and the moon, the tides, and all of the elements."[22]

Enlarging the circle of women's connections to include nature, as Daly did, is the central work of ecofeminists. My work is shaped by the ecofeminist insight that the domination of women and the domination of nature are related injustices. Ecofeminist perspectives inform scholarship in a wide spectrum of fields from religion to literature, natural sciences, philosophy, social sciences, ethnic studies, and history. Although I will discuss the works of Sally Miller Gearhart, Ynestra King, Rosemary Ruether, and Susan Griffin later and I could survey a range of other scholarly works by Vandana Shiva, Joanna Macy, or Paula Gunn Allen, for now I will simply provide Carolyn Merchant's *The Death of Nature* as an exemplary and multidisciplinary analysis of the historical shift toward the mechanistic worldview that supported the exploitation of nature and the subordination of women. Merchant argues that the sixteenth and seventeenth centuries, the Scientific Revolution, saw a decided change in images, ideas, and attitudes associating women and nature. The image of the earth as nurturing mother gradually gave way to the image of nature as wild and uncontrollable (still described in female metaphors).[23] The model of nature as mother curtailed exploitative treatment of the earth, but with diminishing impact of this image, the relationship to nature and to women was modified into one of domination and control. *The Death of Nature* examines art, literature, politics, science, philosophy, and religion as reflections of the new sense of the relationships between culture and nature, women and nature, culture and women, and women and their bodies.

The depth of my work on relationships has been challenged most seriously by women of color. Writing by Chinese-American women has called to my attention the complexity of mother-daughter relationships. Maxine Hong Kingston's autobiography *The Woman Warrior* and Amy Tan's novels *The Joy Luck Club* and *The Kitchen God's Wife* similarly describe the relationships of first generation Chinese-American daughters with their Chinese mothers who immigrated to the United States.[24] Both the autobiographical and fictional accounts of the mother-daughter relationships show the conflict and mystery involved in spanning generations and cultures. The daughters are formed both by bonding with their mothers and by dominant culture in the United States. The resulting tensions created in the stories are a product of internalized racism that makes the daughters critical of and embarrassed by their mothers and that erodes the daughters' sense of personal identity and value. The mother-daughter relationships suffer the effects of racist culture.

African-American writer bell hooks gives critical and constructive insight to the topic of sisterhood in her book *Feminist Theory: From Margin to Center* in which hooks argues that feminist movement has failed to deal with the diversity of women's experiences. I note three significant contributions that hooks has made to theory and political activism that reflect on women's relationships. First, with respect to sisterhood, hooks claims that white feminists experience sisterhood or solidarity based in common victimization.[25] Hooks directs attention to the different basis for solidarity among black women—black women cannot afford sisterhood based in victimization; the solidarity of black women is centered in shared strengths, resources, and political commitment.[26] Second, though critical of white feminism, hooks even states appropriate conditions under which black and white women could experience mutual solidarity—white women must confront their racism, must not attempt to erase the differences among women, and need not experience the same oppression in order to struggle against oppression.[27] Finally, the circle of women's relationships, hooks claims, must include male comrades in the struggle against oppression. Hooks believes that without solidarity with men who are allies in the struggle against sexist oppression, feminist movement is marginalized by its own reactionary separatism.[28] The depth of hooks's theory is a direct result of her breadth of understanding of the diversity and solidarity of women and men who resist oppression.

Womanist literature (as Alice Walker has defined womanist, that is, feminist of color) has captured the theory, experience, psychology, sociology, history, politics, theology, and philosophy of African-American women with unparalleled eloquence. Toni Morrison's *Sula* traces the history of the friendship between Nel Wright and Sula Peace, whose girlhood friendship was so close that they were "two throats and one eye."[29] Neither a romanticization nor an idealization of women's friendship, *Sula* faces squarely the struggles of the friendship as Nel and Sula choose differently how to become African-American women in U.S. culture and as they rage through conflict over Jude, Nel's husband, to reconciliation, until Nel could finally realize and remember, "All that time, all that time, I thought I was missing Jude. . . . We was girls together."[30]

Morrison's *Sula* places female friendship squarely and unflinchingly within the context of complex human relatedness, social and interpersonal, and just as surely Zora Neale Hurston examines the dynamics of female-male relationships in *Their Eyes Were Watching God*.[31] Janie, the focal character of *Their Eyes Were Watching God*, is a woman whose longings and restlessness lead her into three different types of relationships with men. Janie's first marriage to Logan Killicks promises security but threatens to make her little better than the mules on Logan's farm. Janie's second husband, Joe Starks, mayor and store owner in the black town of Eatonville, provides Janie with a very comfortable life but limits her to his ideal of the mayor's wife and imprisons her in a focus on his life. Finally, Janie's third relationship, with Tea Cake, allows her to be simply herself. Working side by side with Tea Cake picking beans, Janie is not dominated by her lover, nor is she the property or reflection of Tea Cake. In her relationship with Tea Cake, Janie's life finally has congruence as her vision of her self, her relationships, and her circumstances become her own and become real.

Alice Walker's *The Color Purple* is so experientially riveting and intellectually brilliant that readers may literally feel womanist theory powerfully told in the fictional story of Celie. *The Color Purple* is certainly a novel about diverse forms of friendship. Celie's relationship with her sister Nettie, as bell hooks might note, is based on shared resources and strengths—Nettie shares her ability to read with Celie; the sisters are committed to protecting each other from their stepfather and from Celie's husband; and through years of separation, they are strengthened by a continuing correspondence that meets no response. Celie's friendship with Shug, her husband's lover, gifts Celie with sexual and spiritual awakening and Shug with health, homecoming, and love. Celie's friendship with Sofia, her stepson's wife, challenges Celie with the Amazonian strength of Sofia's resistance to abuse and racism and supports Sofia during her imprisonment and humiliation by the white establishment. Hardly the romanticizing of female friendship, Celie's friendships are not without conflict when Celie encourages her stepson to beat Sofia and when Shug "betrays" Celie with her male lovers. Surrounded by these friends and Mary Agnes (her stepson's new lover), Celie gains enough courage to confront her husband about his abusive treatment and about hiding Nettie's letters from Celie. Sofia, Shug, and Nettie suggest in their relationships with men a sense of camaraderie that Celie and Mary Agnes learn. Celie and her husband are so transformed in the course of the story that although they do not survive as marriage partners, they do reconcile as friends. Celie's friendships are the context of her metamorphosis—a transformation that leaves no dimension of her life untouched. From Shug, Celie entertains new ways to think of God, nature, and humans as a joyous matrix of connections. Through relationships, Celie discovers empowering ways to experience and name herself in a world where black women are targets of multiple oppressions.

Such a wealth of reflection on relationships is only a selective representation of women's scholarship and experience, but this array of information both dazzles and confounds with the truths that it tells and the tensions that it creates. Although it is tempting to harmonize the riches of women's writings on relationships, it would trivialize and ignore the value of the present works and the potential for further creative work. For the sake of collegiality and creativity, we are bound to struggle with the tensions.

The tensions raised where differing feminist/womanist ideas and experiences interface suggest a number of stimulating questions. First, are there universal statements about women and relationships that appropriately respect the differences among women and their contexts? The literature shows that mother-daughter relationships are not all the same and cannot be isolated from classism and racism. Not all parenting is undertaken in the context of heterosexual households or parenting couples or privatized homes; lesbian and gay couples, single parenting, and extended family and community caregiving certainly exist and offer options for raising children with fewer gender limitations. Class and race differences, in addition to sexual orientation, apparently affect women's senses of the value and justice issues linked to male-female relationships. Even female friendship resists a romantic model of unity.

Second, what are the dynamics of self and community? The locus of feminist revolution ranges from the personal to the interpersonal with some emphasis on relational selfhood. The agency that women have in self-formation is weighed against the influences of parenting whereas the nature of the family is sometimes identified as a shaper of society and sometimes as a product of culture's ethnic, class, religious, political, and gender determinations.

Third, are different forms of oppression analogous? The dominance-subordination model that describes some male-female relationships well is assumed by some authors to be a model that applies equally well to other human oppressions and environmental injustice directly. Womanist literature describes a set of relationships and multiple oppressions that could be described as dominance-subordination but are not necessarily parallel to male-female oppression. Womanist scholarship also adds that the connection between the domination of women and the domination of nature must be understood in the wider context of ethnic and class oppression.

Fourth, does feminist theory internalize gender oppression? Does our interest in writing about relationships or the way that we write reinvent gender oppression? If women are stereotyped as the dependent keepers of relationships, perhaps we strengthen and accept that role in our writing about relationships. Dual parenting could be another way to support the power of males and the dependency of women on male saviors (as Janice Raymond argues).[32] Are we binding women to dependency stereotypes through essentialist or romantic views of relational women?

Sorting out the issues with discernment is no easy matter. A comprehensive framework for connecting and balancing a variety of ideas and experiences, a perspective that facilitates fair criticism and synthesis, could make sense of the tensions. I argue that such a framework must assume that relationships are a given, not just for women, but as a fundamental part of all reality. This philosophical perspective is concerned not with whether there are relations but with what relationships will be—thereby forming the basis for thought and action. I have found the relational philosophy of Alfred North Whitehead to be particularly helpful to me in synthesizing and discerning feminist issues and analysis of relationships.

My thesis is that a constructive feminist theory of relations may be based on the philosophy of Alfred North Whitehead. The organic philosophy of Whitehead is a relational philosophy that complements feminist thought and that may be useful for advancing feminist claims. Although some feminist theorists have discussed relationships from psychological, sociological, historical, or metaphorical standpoints, feminist attempts to propose alternatives to patriarchal or hierarchal relations may be enhanced by the comprehensiveness and cleverness of Whitehead's philosophical perspective. The metaphorical character of some feminist theory and scholarship has sometimes sacrificed or rejected as liabilities both systematization and comprehensiveness. The disadvantage of a strictly metaphorical approach is that the metaphors are rendered vague and ambiguous (even elitist or exclusive) without a context or conceptual framework for their interpretation. Whitehead as philosopher provides a conceptual context; Whitehead as poet suggests metaphors congenial with feminist sensibilities.

Although Whitehead's thought is compatible with feminist thought, it would be inappropriate to use Whitehead's process philosophy uncritically. Mary Daly has described Whitehead's thought as an anticipation of the "dawn of the rising woman-consciousness," but Daly has quite correctly said that Whitehead's philosophy does not address sexism directly, and its purpose does not involve moving outside patriarchal ways of thinking.[33] Daly's warning is that we must beware of prefabricated philosophical theory—our thoughts and words must be our own.[34] Feminism should not use Whitehead's philosophy itself as a feminist philosophy, because it is hardly feminist. Feminist theory may be informed by process philosophy when we are conscious of its limitations and when women's concerns define our agenda.[35] A Whiteheadian feminist voice—a perspective that expresses feminist concerns using Whitehead's conceptuality appropriately—may expand the dimensions of feminism while modifying and extending Whitehead's philosophy. Whitehead's philosophy especially lends itself to the construction of a feminist theory of relations.

Feminism and process philosophy are concerned with relations in a sweeping sense that is inclusive of all types of relationships, from human interrelationships to ecological relationships and the God-world relationship. A preliminary question is, Why is it desirable to make a theory of relations central to philosophy? Why is it important to construct a theory of relations? There are three reasons of significance to the present project (which takes into account both philosophical and theological issues).

First, an ecological perspective has impressed itself upon a contemporary understanding of the world. Since the 1960s, it has become increasingly difficult to think of living things and events as discrete and disconnected. We are becoming more aware that decisions we make about what foods to eat and what products to use directly affect the well-being of other lives and the wider environment. The world is an interconnected web of life that is better understood by reference to its complex relationships than by detailed descriptions of its isolated components. A relational perspective is essential to any scholarship with a concern for the nature and value of the world.

Second, feminism entails a commitment to relationality. Feminism is self-evidently a movement and school of thought originating in discontent with patriarchal, hierarchical relationships. Out of this critical aspect of the movement, feminism has emerged into a constructive enterprise imagining new forms and styles of relating. Although some efforts are directed toward reforming male-female relationships, the most noteworthy constructive work is directed toward repairing the damage that patriarchy has inflicted on woman-woman relationships. The liberation of women (perhaps of humanity and nature as well) lies in restoring mother-daughter and sister-sister relationships. A feminist relational paradigm is crucial as a model for liberating relationships and as a nurturing context for the emergence of women's selfhood.

Third, a theory of relations is theologically and metaphysically important. Sallie McFague has observed that the root-metaphor for Christianity is relational. A root-metaphor is a foundational metaphor that expresses basic assumptions about the nature of reality and experience.[36] McFague appeals to the New Testament parables and the life of Jesus (himself a parable or metaphor for God) as expressions of the kingdom of God which provide Christians with a relational root-metaphor. The kingdom of God is a unique way of being in relationship, and Jesus is the chief exemplar of the Christian mode of relating with God. McFague describes this innovative mode of relationship as an unmerited gift of God's grace that introduces love as the defining characteristic of relationships within the kingdom of God.

> What is critical here is a new quality of relationship, both toward God and toward other human beings. The content of the root-metaphor of Christianity, then, is a mode of personal relationship, exemplified in the parables and with its chief exemplar Jesus himself, a tensive relationship distinguished by trust in God's impossible way of love in contrast to the loveless ways of the world.[37]

If the root-metaphor of Christianity is a quality of relationship exemplified by love within the kingdom of God, then this root-metaphor is a defining and distinguishing mark of Christianity that should be evident in theologies claiming Christian roots. Although all feminist theory is not Christian, I would suggest that relational spiritual models are significantly supportive of feminist praxis.

Believing that it is important to construct different arguments that multiply the voices of women's movement, I approach the construction of a feminist theory of relations as a Whiteheadian feminist. Both feminist and Whiteheadian thought fund my perspective. The relationship of feminism and process thought suggests a number of possible approaches to the current topic. The approach that I have selected is to write as a feminist attempting to persuade a feminist audience that Whitehead's philosophy is a valuable resource for constructing a feminist theory of relations. Other possible approaches are employed incidentally when they further the primary project. Occasionally, as a Whiteheadian, I will explore the limits and extent of the applications and relevance of Whitehead's philosophy to women's experience and feminist theory. At other times, I will construct aspects of a Whiteheadian feminist theory to advance my thesis.

The chapters that follow structure my argument and advance my thesis that Whitehead's philosophy may be a useful basis for a feminist theory of relations. Whitehead's cosmology is employed in the service of experimenting with my feminist cosmology. Chapter 2 outlines what I take to be fundamental aspects of a Whiteheadian feminist theory of relations. This chapter establishes that feminist thought and Whiteheadian philosophy are complementary and that the compatibility between feminism and process philosophy recommends Whitehead as a resource for feminist philosophy and theology. Chapters 3, 4, and 5 continue to advance my thesis in terms of human relationships with nature, human-human relationships, and the God-world relationship. Each chapter discusses the current contributions of feminist thought to its topic and follows with the contributions that Whiteheadian philosophy may add to feminist scholarship. These final chapters demonstrate specifically how Whiteheadian thought supports a feminist theory of relations.

NOTES

1. Nancy Chodorow, *The Reproduction of Mothering: Psychoanalysis and the Sociology of Gender* (Berkeley: University of California Press, 1978), 47, 77.
2. Ibid., 91, 92.
3. Ibid., 7.
4. Ibid., 173.
5. Carol Gilligan, *In a Different Voice: Psychological Theory and Women's Development* (Cambridge: Harvard University Press, 1982), 18, 22.
6. Ibid., 40.
7. Ibid., 105.
8. Jean Baker Miller, *Toward a New Psychology of Women* (Boston: Beacon Press, 1976), 6.
9. Ibid., 69.
10. Ibid., 83.
11. Ibid., 98.
12. Jean Baker Miller, "The Development of Women's Sense of Self," in *Women's Growth in Connection: Writings from the Stone Center*, by Judith V. Jordan, et al. (New York: Guilford Press, 1991), 14.
13. Judith V. Jordan, Janet L. Surrey, and Alexandra G. Kaplan, "Women and Empathy: Implications for Psychological Development and Psychotherapy," in *Women's Growth in Connection: Writings from the Stone Center*, by Judith V. Jordan, et al. (New York: Guilford Press, 1991), 27.
14. Ibid., 31, 38–39.
15. Janet L. Surrey, "The 'Self-in-Relation': A Theory of Women's Development,"

in *Women's Growth in Connection: Writings from the Stone Center*, by Judith V. Jordan, et al. (New York: Guilford Press, 1991), 61; Judith V. Jordan, "The Meaning of Mutuality," in *Women's Growth in Connection: Writings from the Stone Center*, by Judith V. Jordan, et al. (New York: Guilford Press, 1991), 82.

16. Irene P. Stiver, "The Meanings of 'Dependency' in Female-Male Relationships," in *Women's Growth in Connection: Writings from the Stone Center*, by Judith V. Jordan, et al. (New York: Guilford Press, 1991), 160.

17. Janet L. Surrey, "Relationship and Empowerment," in *Women's Growth in Connection: Writings from the Stone Center*, by Judith V. Jordan, et al. (New York: Guilford Press, 1991), 168.

18. Janice G. Raymond, *A Passion for Friends: Toward a Philosophy of Female Affection* (Boston: Beacon Press, 1986), 8.

19. Mary E. Hunt, *Fierce Tenderness: A Feminist Theology of Friendship* (New York: Crossroad, 1991), 8.

20. Ibid., 29.

21. Ibid., 98.

22. Mary Daly, *Pure Lust: Elemental Feminist Philosophy* (Boston: Beacon Press, 1984), 311.

23. Carolyn Merchant, *The Death of Nature: Women, Ecology, and the Scientific Revolution* (San Francisco: Harper & Row, 1980), 2.

24. Maxine Hong Kingston, *The Woman Warrior: Memoirs of a Girlhood among Ghosts* (New York: Random House; Vintage Books, 1977); Amy Tan, *The Joy Luck Club* (New York: Ballantine Books; Ivy Books, 1989); Amy Tan, *The Kitchen God's Wife* (New York: Ballantine Books; Ivy Books, 1991).

25. bell hooks, *Feminist Theory: From Margin to Center* (Boston: South End Press, 1984), 45.

26. Ibid.

27. Ibid., 55, 65.

28. Ibid., 71.

29. Toni Morrison, *Sula* (New York: New American Library; Plume Book, 1973), 147.

30. Ibid., 174.

31. Zora Neale Hurston, *Their Eyes Were Watching God* (Urbana and Chicago: University of Illinois Press, 1978).

32. Janice G. Raymond, "Female Friendship: Contra Chodorow and Dinnerstein," *Hypatia* 1 no. 2 (Fall 1986): 37–48.

33. Mary Daly, *Beyond God the Father: Toward a Philosophy of Women's Liberation* (Boston: Beacon Press, 1973), 188–89.

34. Ibid.

35. One feminist criticism of Whitehead concerns the fact that contemporaries do not participate in an internal relationship. The relationships among contemporaries are external. This means that in Whitehead's system, the doctrine of internal relations is primarily concerned with subject-object relations rather than intersubjective relationships. A feminist theory of relations should include intersubjective relationships as part of its foundational understanding of relations.
    A second feminist criticism of Whitehead is that his cosmology entails a hierarchy. I will advance this criticism in detail in chapter 3.

36. Sallie McFague, *Metaphorical Theology: Models of God in Religious Language* (Philadelphia: Fortress Press, 1982), 28.

37. Ibid., 108.

CONSTRUCTING A FEMINIST COSMOLOGY

FEMINISTS HAVE ENTERED A productive period in which constructive attempts at postpatriarchal theories of relations are being formulated and imaged in light of women's experience and ideas. My contention is that a promising feminist theory of relations, a feminist ecological cosmology, may be supported and informed by Alfred North Whitehead's cosmology. The basis of this thesis is that there is complementarity between Whiteheadian philosophy and feminist thought from which emerges a theory of relations adequate to promote a radical reconstruction of ecological, human, and metaphysical relations. Whitehead's doctrine of internal relations supports and advances women's new visions of interrelationships. Suggesting the potential for a Whiteheadian feminist cosmology, however, involves both positive and negative evaluation of process philosophy from the perspective of feminist thought and women's experiences. Hierarchical features of Whitehead's philosophy especially should be modified in response to feminist concerns.

Constructive feminist energies have recently been directed toward imaging feminist theories of relations. From Mary Daly's description of Be-Friending in *Pure Lust* to Janice Raymond's construction of a feminist philosophy of female friendship in *A Passion for Friends*, feminist theorists have created—and remembered—relational worldviews that reflect the importance of sisterhood as a paradigm for interconnectedness. For other feminists, critical analysis of patriarchal modes of relating and the experience of sisterhood as an alternate mode of relating have led to confrontation of hierarchical structures of relations. Women have chosen to address the hetero-relational problematic directly by suggesting a reconstruction of female-male relationships (see, for example, Margaret Farley's *Personal Commitments*[1]). Reflecting beyond humanocentric relationships, women are equally concerned with women's connection with nature. The centrality of the issue of the connection of humans and nature is pervasive, but it is especially evident in ecofeminism, a vital movement among women for environmental justice (including such practical theorists as Charlene Spretnak, author of *The Spiritual Dimension of Green Politics*[2]).

A general interest among women in the construction of a feminist theory

13

of relations, however, does not reflect a consensus. Instead, it reflects the diversity of women's perspectives apparent in all areas of feminism. Especially with respect to the topic of relationality, diversity of images and ideas not only should be expected but encouraged as a contribution to the multiversity. Radical change in the dominant patriarchal pattern of relationships may require the suggestion of a multiplicity of alternatives to male-defined hierarchy. A variety of concrete options will be necessary for opening the way to real, novel possibilities in human relating.

I find it useful that the philosophy of organism constructed by Alfred North Whitehead provides a framework for a feminist theory of relations. An overarching reason for experimenting with process philosophy as a contribution to feminist construction of a new view of relations is that it provides a cosmology radically different from dominant mechanistic and patriarchal worldviews. I suggest that it is inadequate to work, however critically, within the dominant worldview. A change in worldview will more adequately take account of and emerge from feminist concerns. In addition, a new worldview will be necessary to effect the radical changes required by feminism. Although process philosophy is not a prefabricated feminist theory of relations, it provides a worldview that is compatible with feminist perspectives in several respects, and the complementarity of feminism and process philosophy suggests the fruitfulness of Whiteheadian metaphors for feminist theory.

My cosmology is an experiment. Intellectually and experientially, my Whiteheadian feminist cosmology is a synthetic process of sorting through feminist/womanist relational principles, then organizing and connecting them with the assistance of Whitehead's cosmological framework. From the complementarity of Whitehead's cosmology with feminist/womanist relational perspectives, the following principles are emerging as central to my feminist cosmology.

A Conceptual Interpretation of Women's Experiences

A feminist cosmology best interprets women's experiences in terms of relational, organic thinking, and Whitehead's philosophy is a helpful conceptual framework.

When feminists have spoken personally about the relevance of Whitehead's philosophy to women's experience, their reasons for relating process thought to feminism have been grounded in conceptual and experiential intuitions. Valerie Saiving found in process thought a conceptual framework for her emerging feminism. Following the awakening of her feminist consciousness, Saiving found that process philosophy provided a conceptual framework within which to interpret the profound transformations taking place in her life. Whitehead's philosophy suggested an androgynous vision that confronted the nonandrogynous ideal that had previously shaped Saiving's life. The coincidence of feminist awareness and process thought led Saiving to draw two conclusions.

On the one hand, not even an intimate acquaintance with Whitehead's ideas is capable of *creating* feminist consciousness; such consciousness arises out of certain kinds of life experience, explored in dialogue with other women. On the other hand, feminist consciousness, once awakened, seeks a conceptual framework for self-understanding, and process philosophy may provide such a framework.[3]

Similarly, Penelope Washbourn experienced process thought as an encouragement for her feminist questing.

It was process thought that taught me to be a feminist, certainly it was process thought that taught me to be interested in questions concerning women and religion. Perhaps I could say now in retrospect that my being drawn to the study and development of a process mode of thinking may also have been related to an unconscious awareness that it offered me not only a more viable theological and philosophical framework than any other, but also an opportunity to integrate my identity as a woman within a religious framework.[4]

Marjorie Suchocki discovered an experiential identification with Whitehead's philosophy. Whitehead was a philosopher who seemed to have experienced the world in much the same way that Suchocki had, and his perception of the nature and dynamics of the world was expressed in a comprehensive metaphysics that seemed meaningful to Suchocki in light of her experience. In a personal sense, Suchocki subjected Whitehead's philosophy to the criterion of fit with women's experience and concluded, "I come to it not as an interesting speculative system, though it is surely that, but from my need to understand my world in holistic terms through a conceptuality which fits my experience."[5]

My experience is similar to Saiving's, Washbourn's, and Suchocki's. The coincidence of my feminist awakening with my discovery of Whitehead's relational philosophy supported my experience of myself and my relationships. Not accidentally or surprisingly, it is out of this experience that my feminist cosmology emerges with clear Whiteheadian and feminist underpinnings.

Thus, the compatibility of feminism and process thought rests in two dimensions. First, process thought "rings true" to women's experiences by virtue of its comprehensive ability to take account of women's experiences. Second, process thought provides a conceptuality within which women may understand and interpret their experiences. Although Whitehead's process philosophy is not a feminist philosophy, it may contribute one interpretive tool to women who desire a holistic understanding of women's experience.

EXPERIENCE AS FUNDAMENTAL

A feminist cosmology must entertain the widest range of experience possible as its data, especially diverse women's experiences.

Methodologically, experience is the feature that links process philosophy and feminist thought. Valerie Saiving recognized that Whitehead affirmed the expansiveness of experience both in his epistemology and in his conceptuality itself, whereas Mary Daly's assessment of process philosophy is more reserved. Daly's affirmation of process philosophy in *Beyond God the Father* prefaced the warning that women must beware of easy acquiescence to prefabricated theory, because the essential aim of feminist theology/philosophy is to elicit, express, and interpret women's experience.[6] Valerie Saiving has noted, however, that the sentiment expressed by Daly is present in Whitehead. In the first place, the experiencing subject is the primary datum for process metaphysics.[7] In the second place, Whitehead himself held no allegiance to systems at the expense of experience. In *Modes of Thought*, Whitehead praised William James for the character of his intellectual life, which was "one protest against the dismissal of experience in the interest of system."[8] In addition, Whitehead was willing to work within a philosophical framework without being imprisoned by it. Recall, also from *Modes of Thought*, that Whitehead lamented the fact that there are traps in the pursuit of learning. It is easy to become consumed by details that lead us into closed systems of thought and blindness to the limitations of those systems. In this passage, Whitehead reminded us of an important principle—"In order to acquire learning, we must first shake ourselves free of it"—and, through a criticism of John Stuart Mill, Whitehead explained that the danger is that we may inherit a "system before any enjoyment of the relevant experience."[9] These priorities advocated by Whitehead are relevant for feminist theorists (even for those of us who look to Whitehead for philosophical suggestions). Experience precedes theory.

Whitehead's criticism of substantialist philosophies led him to broaden the range of experience included in his metaphysics. Hence, Whitehead insisted upon the inclusion of every variety of experience. One passage from *Adventures of Ideas* is often quoted to indicate the infinite range of experience to which Whitehead referred.

> In order to discover some of the major categories under which we can classify the infinitely various components of experience, we must appeal to evidence relating to every variety of occasion. Nothing must be omitted, experience drunk and experience sober, experience sleeping and experience waking, experience drowsy and experience wide-awake, experience self-conscious and experience self-forgetful, experience intellectual and experience physical, experience religious and experience sceptical, experience

anxious and experience care-free, experience anticipatory and experience retrospective, experience happy and experience grieving, experience dominated by emotion and experience under self-restraint, experience in the light and experience in the dark, experience normal and experience abnormal.[10]

The lengthy list of experiences that comprise this passage suggests the diversity and intensity of experiences to which philosophy must be held accountable. If Whitehead can be taken seriously here, feminists must conclude that the range of experiences that funds philosophy includes women's experience. Making this point explicitly, Valerie Saiving has added "experience female and experience male" to Whitehead's list.[11]

The inclusiveness of the experience that Whitehead wished to embrace in his philosophy was affirmed earlier in *Process and Reality*: "Philosophy may not neglect the multifariousness of the world—the fairies dance, and Christ is nailed to the cross."[12] Narrowness in the selection of experiential evidence for philosophy results in serious distortions, and this evil is born of several sources.

This narrowness arises from the idiosyncrasies and timidities of particular authors, of particular social groups, of particular schools of thought, of particular epochs in the history of civilization. The evidence relied upon is arbitrarily biased by the temperaments of individuals, by the provincialities of groups, and by the limitations of schemes of thought.[13]

Feminists would support this statement by reference to patriarchal philosophies that are narrow and limited by virtue of the exclusion of women's experience from their range of data. It is also inadequate for women's experience to be co-opted into patriarchal schemes of thought that preserve system at the expense of experience. The unjustified exclusiveness and narrowness of experiential evidence is not merely to be augmented by the inclusion of other experiences (for example, women's experience). An inclusive philosophy is urged beyond the status quo in fashioning ideals by movement between two contrasts—permanence and flux, order and novelty. This movement suggests that the result of being inclusive of the vast range of experiences is a dynamic philosophy that promotes and reflects change.

As a Whiteheadian feminist, I am situated clearly among white, educated, middle-class feminists. Womanists who criticize white U.S. feminist scholarship as elitist and racist have easily convinced me that their charges are painfully well founded—and in the process, womanists have shaped me as a better scholar and Whiteheadian. I had carefully applied Whitehead's admonition to be inclusive of experience to the addition of women's experience to male experience. I had righteously pointed out the narrowness of patriarchal systems. Unfortunately, I had also simplemindedly made universal assumptions about women's experience. Womanists and Whitehead hold me accountable to the particularity of diverse women's experiences. I am charged to craft a feminist cosmology that is most inclusive of women's experience without co-opting womanist experience, which would be supremacist in womanist terms and a case of evil in Whitehead's.

IMPORTANCE AND FEMINIST LOGIC

A feminist cosmology is crafted within the subjective experience of particular women and should avoid making universal claims.

In contrast to patriarchal methodologies based on logical argumentation and reasoning (sometimes in abstraction from the concrete), Whitehead and feminist theorists advocate a "new logic" based on experience. Along with the general significance of experience, however, Whitehead also discussed a valuable dimension of experience that he referred to as "importance." Importance and matter of fact are two contrasting and complementary aspects of experience. Concentration is focused on matters of fact, because we sense the relative importance of the facts.[14] The multiplicity of matters of fact requires the capacity to select from among an incomprehensible amount of data. The process of selection is an exercise of intellectual freedom.[15] Importance is not merely interest—the intensity of individual feeling for details—because importance is more concerned with the "unity of the Universe." The idea of importance suggests breadth and the wider connection of details, while it recognizes that a particular perspective is applied to matters of fact.[16]

The connection between experience and importance reflects an issue of concern to feminists. Much scholarship has been characterized by the sense that studies deal in an objective way with matters of fact. This suggests a universality in scholarly conclusions that is not always justified. As Whitehead observes, the range of matters of fact which one can consider is limited by the finitude of the intellect. It is not improper to limit one's selection of the facts to be considered; however, it is improper to assume that one has not imposed a perspective upon the consideration of those facts or that one has exhausted the range of data available for consideration. The overarching criticism that women bring to patriarchal scholarship is that it refuses to acknowledge that it exercises this selective process and that its perspective is decidedly masculine. A blindness to the perspectival nature of scholarship has led to the assumption that it speaks universally when it has eliminated reference to women's experiences and consequently subjects women to masculine norms.

The criticism of traditional male scholarship may serve as a warning to feminists that they must be diligent about acknowledging women's perspectives.

For the most part, women are conscious about the deliberate selection of women's experience as the data from which they work. In fact, women scholars are frequently identified by the way in which they select and use matters of fact. Sallie McFague's classification of women theologians as either revolutionists or reformers is an example of identification based on importance. Revolutionists select women's experience as data for theology, but reformers include liberating motifs from the Christian tradition. Both groups acknowledge a perspective. Revolutionists do not identify themselves as Christian (they may describe themselves as postchristian), although reformers identify themselves as Christians. Revolutionists are concerned with women's liberation and evaluate theology based on what fits and enhances women's experience. Reformers are concerned with male and female liberation and evaluate theology based on the potential for liberation within the Christian tradition.[17]

In addition to these two basic distinctions addressed by McFague, feminists have also learned to be conscious that an individual woman may not speak on behalf of all women. In other words, to the extent that women exercise what Whitehead calls interest, women remain conscious of their individual racial, ethnic, socioeconomic diversity. This has led, for example, to the distinction between white feminist scholarship and womanist scholarship and the appropriate criticism that white feminists have made universal claims about women. The logic of importance moves my feminist cosmology beyond interest in my particular context to seek breadth and connections among diverse particular women's experiences. Whitehead's "unity of the Universe" requires that I consider the differences in women's experiences, that I understand their complex connections, and that I respect and retain their particularity in the unity implied by relationships.

EXPERIENCE AND THOUGHT

A feminist cosmology, as a theory of relations, reflects on experience and inspires praxis.

Another methodological connection between feminist theory and Whiteheadian philosophy is a sense of the necessary connection between experience or action and reflection. Feminist theology/philosophy is identified with liberation movements and shares an emphasis on praxis. Letty Russell, a feminist whose methodology directly parallels that of Latin American liberation theology, describes praxis as an essential dimension of liberation theology. Liberation theology is meant to be practiced, so our scholarship is a combination of theory and practice. Russell describes praxis as "action that is concurrent with reflection or analysis and leads to new questions, actions, and reflections."[18] This definition indicates the intimate connection between action and reflection—it is a constant cycle of action and reflection that describes experience/action as a resource for reflection and theory-reflection as a resource for action.

In *Black Feminist Thought*, Patricia Hill Collins writes about the relationship of thought and action. Collins argues that black feminist thought rejects the dichotomy between thought and action. In contrast to either–or thinking, both–and thinking expands the efficacy of thought and action. The relationship of thought and action means that a change in thought, consciousness, and self-definition changes action. For black women, changes in self-definition—changes that are a refusal to be defined by the dominant culture—fire acts of resistance and political activism.[19]

The connection between experience and reflection is also evident in Sallie McFague's concern for the relationship between the concrete and the abstract in her study of religious language. Language must represent the relationship between experience and theory. McFague relates metaphor to our concrete experience. It is metaphor that connects language directly with experience. In fact, all language is metaphorical in that metaphor funds thought and knowledge. Metaphor funds conceptual language, but metaphor is not itself theory, abstraction, or concept. For this reason, metaphor and concept require a mediator. This mediator between the concrete and the abstract is a model. Models (which are dominant metaphors) have the imagistic character of metaphor and the organizing intelligibility of concepts.[20] Experience and reflection in religious language are connected by McFague's proposal that models connect the experiential aspect of language, metaphor, with the reflective aspect that is conceptual or theological language.

What Russell has done with praxis, what Collins has done with self-definition toward resistance, and what McFague has done with models to connect experience and reflection have a parallel in Whitehead. For Whitehead, the connection between action and reflection has more than methodological implications, because Whitehead gives this connection an ontological status. The most basic aspect of Whitehead's philosophy is the explanation of the role of process in the real world. One dimension of process (or creativity) is what he calls transition. Transition is a sequential creative advance from actualities in the past to the emergence of the present actuality which then joins the multiplicity of past actualities in contributing to the emergence of future actualities. Predominantly, this process occurs apart from conscious reflection, but if we focus on instances when self-reflection is possible, then we can see how action and reflection are related in Whitehead's scheme.

The actualities in the past are those matters of fact to which I referred earlier. Consciously or unconsciously, emerging actualities must select from the multiplicity of matters of fact those that will have significance for their emergence. Most of these "decisions" are a product of habit, but a minority involves a conscious determination of which data will be eliminated and which will be constitutive of the present moment. These decisions concern the issue of importance (mentioned previously), and they are a component of reflection that leads to the development of philosophy, theology, and even feminist theory. In the Whiteheadian schema, these matters of fact function much more significantly than as mere objects of data for consideration. The conscious selection or elimination of matters of fact is only one way to take account of past data. We are intimately related to those matters of fact, so that not only do we reflect upon them, but they are formative of the present.[21] In other words, my thoughts partially form the person who I am becoming in the present.

The reflection of the feminist theorist is not just an intellectual exercise—it actually makes her the zealous activist. The ideological commitments of all persons contribute to their formation. Feminist consciousness raising (or similarly conscientization, in the term familiar to Latin American liberationists) is a good example of this process. Consciousness raising, in changing the way women think of themselves, their relationships, and their aspirations, changes the behavior and political action of women. Additionally, a feminist commitment to gender inclusive language assumes that thought and the mode of expressing ideas in language affect human behavior. We wait with eager anticipation to verify that changing language changes attitudes and practices. The connection of experience and reflection in feminist theory is analogous to Whitehead's ontological connection of experience and thought such that Whitehead's philosophy may be a fruitful advocate in articulating those claims.

DUALISM

A feminist cosmology resists classical dualism.

In addition to the priority of experience in process philosophy, many feminists have noted the importance of Whitehead's attempt to overcome classical dualism. Mary Daly first noted, in *Beyond God the Father*, that Whitehead eliminated the Creator/creature dichotomy by replacing the notion of God the Creator with the view that God is with all creation. Daly described Whitehead's thought as a unity of technical and ontological reason, intended to overcome the dualism of intellectuality and shallow objective consciousness. In addition, Daly pointed toward the encouraging character of Whitehead's denial of the duality of purposive human existence and nonpurposive nature.[22]

More recently, Dorothee Soelle has recognized the promise of process philosophy for a nondualistic theology of creation. Soelle has suggested that the traditional distinction between God and the world is captured in a set of "godly"/"worldly" dualisms—Creator/Created, Lord/Servant, Maker/Made, Artist/Artifact, Will or form/Stuff or matter, Cause/Effect, Subject/Object.

The problem with the supposedly unbridgeable gap between the creator and the created is that it has been transposed, for example, into sexist dichotomizing, in which we ascribe "godly" characteristics to the male and "worldly" characteristics to the female. The ontological concept is used in a sexist sense. Indeed, many injurious dichotomies flow out of our positing an unequivocal separation between God and humanity. Must we subscribe to this imperialistic concept of creation? Is there not a different way of construing creation and the relationship between God and the world?[23]

Soelle's obvious answer is that there is a way to overcome the God/world dichotomy (and attendant dualisms) through a nonimperialistic reconception of God. Soelle has credited Whitehead and process thinkers with the advancement of one option that images God as dynamic and relational with respect to the world.

There are many dualisms reinterpreted by Whiteheadian thought in such a way that they minimize sexist dichotomizing. An important dichotomy is subject/object dualism, which feminist analysis cites frequently as the basis for objectification of women and nature. In Whitehead's thought, we have the basis for thinking of each actuality as both subject and object. In its emergence, each actuality is an experiencing subject with the capacity for self-determination. In its actualization, each actuality is an object, datum, or matter of fact experienced by other actualities. It is possible with Whitehead's metaphysics to think of persons (who are societies of actualities) as both subjects and objects. Persons are capable of experiencing others and of being experienced by others. Persons are both means and ends with respect to their value.

Persons are also psychosomatic wholes, not to be fragmented into a dichotomized body and mind. Traditionally this dichotomy has been used as a basis for the identification of woman with the body and of man with the mind, but in Whitehead's thought, the radical intimacy or dependence of body and mind makes this segregation unlikely. John B. Cobb Jr. has developed one Whiteheadian interpretation of personal psychosomatic unity in which he notes the interrelatedness of body, psyche, and spirit. Cobb notes that we are well aware of this interdependence of the aspects of the psychosomatic whole whenever physical ill health affects, for example, the emotional well-being of the whole person.[24]

A final example is the dichotomy of reason and emotions. On the basis of this dichotomy, men have stereotypically been described as rational, and women have been described as emotional. Whitehead provides a perspective from which to see that reason and emotion are integrated aspects of persons. Emerging actualities take account of past data in their constitution. Whitehead uses the terms "prehension" and "feeling" to name this act. Within Whitehead's schema, both reason and emotion are involved in prehending or feeling the objective data. Consciousness and emotions are two subjective forms or ways of feeling the data.[25] Reason and emotion need not be considered two oppositional, mutually exclusive approaches to the world but two of a number of equally important ways of responding to the world.

CHANGE

A feminist cosmology describes reality as processive and dynamic.

For both Whitehead and feminists, change and dynamism are essential. In part, Soelle's positive assessment of process philosophy embraces the idea of process and dynamism itself, and she recognizes this aspect in process philosophy as an aspect of Whitehead's thought that is compatible with feminism. Soelle highlights the importance of becoming as an ontological category in contrast to being as the foundational category of existence. Becoming-ontology gives priority to process instead of substance and thereby affords a more suitable conceptuality for a theology of creation. Becoming-ontology also lifts relationships into centrality; so that events, life, and life's processes constitute reality in its interrelatedness.[26] This compatibility points toward four features of Whitehead's philosophy: actual occasions, concrescence, transition, and internal relationships.

First, the actualities to which I have referred are variously called actual occasions, actual entities, indivisible events, or droplets of experience by Whitehead. If you can imagine, these discrete moments of experience are very small, like the precise childhood instant when we first connect a word to the letters of the alphabet that spell the word. Think also of all the discrete moments that preceded and enabled making that connection: instants that are part of making infant sounds, learning words one by one, having thousands of stories read at bedtime, singing the alphabet. These ordinary and extraordinary instants, actual occasions, are the *res verae* in Whitehead's categoreal scheme.[27] Events are the fundamental units of reality, the final realities. This means that reality may best be understood in terms of experience and relationships. This claim requires a major shift from thinking of reality as composed primarily of substances to thinking of reality in terms of experience or events. Whiteheadian scholars recognize the difficulty in making this shift in thinking. Anne Wilson Schaef has noticed a very similar contrast in the White Male System and the Female System:

> The White Male System feels the need to analyze, understand, and explain the world. It does so by taking a whole, breaking it down into its component parts, and defining each of these parts in turn. People and things are seen as being however they are defined.
> The Female System sees the world as constantly growing and changing. It cannot be defined; it can only be observed as it emerges. Understanding

comes from watching, learning from, and facilitating the process of emergence.[28]

Both process philosophy and the Female System have in common a focus upon emergence. They approach the world as a process rather than a static entity.

Second, each individual actual occasion is the process of actuality emerging out of potentiality. An actual occasion is a concrescence, the process of unification of a universe of potentialities in a single instance. Concrescence is the act of becoming that is effected by prehension or feeling of the multiplicity of matters of fact. For example, the one moment when I first heard the word "cat" and indelibly realized its representation in the letters C-A-T was the concrescence or drawing together of a history of discrete moments of learning sounds, seeing cats, singing ABCs, and hearing the word "cat." My potential to read the word "cat" became actual as I intuitively felt and consciously remembered thousands of tiny events in my life. Concrescence as a relational process of connecting events constitutes an actual occasion.[29] The idea of concrescence is central to Whitehead's understanding of process or creativity, and it is intimately related to transition.

Transition (which has already been mentioned) is the third dimension of the creative process that involves the temporal passage from actual occasion to actual occasion. Transition occurs by means of prehension or feeling. An experiencing subject feels initial data (the multiplicity of data). As certain data are eliminated, the initial data concresce into the objective datum in connection with the subjective form (how the data are felt).[30] The concrescing actual occasion in its self-determination reaches completion or satisfaction, and the process begins again for another becoming occasion as the previous one is added to the multiplicity. This is the movement from past to present to future. The present is constituted by the past and contributes itself as a datum for the future. Returning to my example, a connected history of events involved transition from first seeing a cat, then hearing it called "cat," to subsequent repeated cat sightings and naming, to saying "cat" for the first time, to hearing my first story about a cat, to the much later first grade C-A-T/"cat" revelation—astoundingly the C-A-T moment was early in the chain of connected moments leading to college, graduate school, and writing this book. This progression of events and making connections was facilitated by positive, curious, playful, daring emotional feelings that enabled movement from one stage to the next. Concrescence and transition are descriptions of internal and external forms of change, both of which have relevance to feminist experience, desire for personal transformation, and hope for social change.

The fourth factor is relationality. Relationality is the point of the most dramatic correspondence of feminist theory and Whiteheadian philosophy. Anne Wilson Schaef has referred to relationality as the "center of the universe" for the Female System.[31] It is no less than the center of the universe for Whitehead. Because of its importance, Whitehead's doctrine of internal relations will be discussed in the next section.

RELATIONS

A feminist cosmology entails a concept of internal relations.

Because process philosophy is essentially a relational philosophy, it has in common with feminism an emphasis upon the interconnectedness of persons and of humans with nature. Feminism, particularly with respect to female friendship or sisterhood, has felt the importance of interrelatedness for each individual self-actualization. The doctrine of internal relations in process thought suggests a philosophical interpretation of the importance of relationships for the becoming of an individual event, including a person-in-the-making.

Internal relations are distinct from external relations in that they are essential for the creation and existence of events, although external relations are not essential to the character of the events (or substances) to which they usually refer. In external relations, substances first exist and then enter into relationships, and the essential nature of a substance is not affected by its relations. Internal relations are those relationships that constitute both living and nonliving events with respect to their character and existence. Events owe their very existence to a particular occurrence of relationships within a spatiotemporal location. Examples? A strict believer in external relations might say that the cat, the book with the word "cat," and the first-grade child are independent of each other and that each would be what it is apart from the others. A believer in internal relations would say that the child is what she is because of her encounter with the cat and the book and that even the cat and the book are changed because of their relationships with the child.

Internal relations are instrumental in the creative process. Creativity is instantiated in each event when through internal relations the many become one and are increased by one. Each concrescing event is a subject that prehends or feels the past. The concrescing event creates itself in freedom by taking account of objective data from the past and a divine persuasive lure toward rich experience that influence the way in which an event constitutes itself. When the event concresces as an actual occasion, it contributes to the actualization of future events. Translated from Whiteheadian, this means that the first-grade Nancy was surrounded by cats, books, alphabets, sounds, and encouraging adults, as well as a divine presence that beckoned her to meet the challenge of connecting "cat" with C-A-T. Not particularly obstinate, the playful and curious Nancy welcomed these influences to become a part of herself and to create a "new" Nancy, a fully reading Nancy. That tiny reader no longer exists, but she is now one influence from the wealth of historical moments creating the current Nancy Howell, Ph.D., who sits here revising and writing a text. This creative process is my childhood, my present writing challenge, and my hope for future dialogue with colleagues.

Beverly Harrison has applied this philosophical perspective to a feminist interpretation of creativity, freedom, and relationality. Associating relationality and power, this application illustrates that a feminist perspective on power, which in fact is understood as empowerment, can be based on Whiteheadian philosophy.

> In feminist terms, God is not the One who stands remotely in control, but the One who binds us and bids us to deep relationality, resulting in a radical equality motivated by genuine mutuality and interdependence. In a community transformed by this utopian vision, power would be experienced as *reciprocity in relation*. In other words, our individual power to act would be nourished and enhanced by mutual regard and cocreativity.
>
> Freedom, when understood as the power of creativity, achieves its consummate expression in deepened community.... To be free means possessing the power to imaginatively interact with others, to give and to receive, to act upon and to suffer (that is, to be acted upon), to participate with others in cocreating a world.[32]

Harrison empowers sisterhood with the suggestion that freedom is the power of creativity. The power of creativity is not diminished by interconnectedness, because it is a power rooted in relationality, mutuality, and cocreativity. This is an empowerment born of the relationships of women with each other and with God.

Whiteheadian feminist Catherine Keller has applied the doctrine of internal relations to the patriarchal problem of separate and soluble selves. The separate self is the illusion that persons are discrete, disconnected, autonomous selves (for example, the "self-made man"). The soluble self is the stereotypical role of women in patriarchy that binds and dissolves women into the role of relationship-makers and relationship-keepers. Whitehead's doctrine of internal relations provides a conceptuality for relational selfhood that arises from a multitude of relationships (indeed, the person herself is a society). Keller has argued that this conceptuality affirms both relationality and selfhood while eliminating the dualistic choice between soluble selfhood and separate selfhood.[33] Keller (like Jean Baker Miller and other Stone Center scholars) urges that we understand ourselves as relational selves.

The organic worldview weaves together the concepts of internal relations, subjectivity, freedom, creativity, and prehension (feeling). The doctrine of internal relations has the potential for additional fruitful applications and expressions of feminist concerns.

NATURE

A feminist cosmology values nature and its interconnections.
An important parallel between Whitehead and feminism is an extraordinary appreciation for the cosmos. For both, nature is valued for its diversity and subjectivity. In process thought and feminist thought, humans experience kinship and continuity with nature.

The intimate sense of connection that women feel with nature is expressed in a number of ways. Frequently, women's relationship with nature can be expressed with nothing less than the word "sisterhood," which not only notes a connection with nature but establishes that relationship on the basis of equality.[34]

Claims about the intimate relationship of women and nature are especially evident in writings by women who are pantheists, goddess religionists, and Wicca practioners. These feminists express the radical relatedness of nature, deity, and women reflected in Alice Walker's *The Color Purple*. In a frequently quoted passage, Walker creates a dialogue about God between her main characters Shug and Celie, in which Shug talks about her realization of these connections: "I knew that if I cut a tree, my arm would bleed."[35] This feeling for nature is not merely a literary device; it reflects a pivotal value among feminist theorists. For example, Susan Griffin, in *Woman and Nature*, expresses the same theme in a passage called "The Earth: What She Means to Me":

> She is as delicate as I am; I know her sentience; I feel her pain and my own pain comes into me, and my own pain grows large and I grasp this pain with my hands, and I open my mouth to this pain, I taste, I know, and I know why she goes on, under great weight, with this great thirst, in drought, in starvation, with intelligence in every act does she survive disaster. This earth is my sister; I love her daily grace, her silent daring, and how loved I am *how we admire this strength in each other, all that we have lost, all that we have suffered, all that we know: we are stunned by this beauty,* and I do not forget: what she is to me, what I am to her.[36]

What Griffin reflects with a feminist perspective is a sisterhood with nature that entails mutuality between women and nature. Women share and feel the suffering of nature, just as nature shares and feels the suffering of women. It is a focus on intense interdependence between women and nature.

This interdependence is also the basis of the common view among feminists that women's struggle for liberation is conjoined with the campaign for environmental justice. In fact, Sharon Doubiago has claimed that feminism and ecology are the same subject, two inseparable fields of study.[37] Behind Doubiago's comment is the feminist perspective that the oppression and consequently the liberation of women and nature are intertwined. Judith Plant expresses this claim that is central to ecofeminism: women and nature suffer the same oppression, and the liberation of nature and women is a single movement.

> Since women have been associated with nature, with all that is natural, in taking a stand on the war on nature and by confronting the oppression of the earth, we confront the oppression of ourselves.[38]

The oppression of women and nature is a result of their identification. Liberation of women and nature, therefore, requires an ecofeminist assault upon that oppression.

Whitehead offers some related insights from a philosophical perspective. The first that will be mentioned here is that there is continuity between humans and nature. This is an insight that is common not only to feminists and ecologists but to process philosophy. The relational worldview proposed by Whitehead applies to all experience whether divine, human, or nonhuman. Nature, then, is a part of reality understood in terms of events or actual occasions. All nature is best described as actual occasions and as experiencing subjects with some capacity for self-creativity within a network of constitutive internal relations. Whitehead describes the difference between humans and animals as a difference of degree (with respect to feeling and expression).[39] Although Whitehead would want to note the significance of that difference in degree, it is evident that clear and rigid boundaries do not segregate aspects of nature itself and that humans and nature are not sharply separated.

A second feature of Whitehead's thought, which suggests that nature has significant status in process philosophy, is that the term "person" is redefined to include animals. All living bodies, including humans, animals, and vegetables, are societies of actual occasions, but the continuous temporal societies of animals and humans are characterized by an internal organizer that acts as a social coordinator of the society of occasions that make up the living body.[40] The sequence of these occasions is what Whitehead calls a living person or a soul. Humans and most animals, especially vertebrates, have this internal organizer or social coordinator that Whitehead referred to as the presiding or dominant occasion of experience.[41] Whitehead's view of reality offers this basis for interpreting the kinship of humans and nature. Whitehead's philosophy of personality and his doctrine of internal relations combine to describe the independence and interdependence of nature and humanity.

NONTRADITIONAL THEISM

A feminist cosmology entertains postmodern metaphysics and rejects classical theism.

Of further interest to feminists is the postmodern understanding of God proposed by process philosophy. God is a participant in the reality described by the dynamic process ontology. God is in relationship, not incidentally or accidentally, but essentially. As such, aseity is no longer a viable descriptor for God, because every action is an interaction which implies change. Potentiality is appropriate to God's experience in itself and to God's influence on free entities. In the dynamic character of God is the capacity to affect and to be affected. Thus, it is meaningful to speak of mutuality and interrelatedness between God and the world.

With respect to the formulation of an understanding of God, Whitehead and feminists are united in the creative effort to supersede classical theism. In *Process and Reality*, Whitehead explicitly rejected the idea of God as ruling Caesar, ruthless moralist, and unmoved mover for the Galilean vision.

> There is, however, in the Galilean origin of Christianity yet another suggestion which does not fit very well with any of the three main strands of thought. It does not emphasize the ruling Caesar, or the ruthless moralist, or the unmoved mover. It dwells upon the tender elements in the world, which slowly and in quietness operate by love; and it finds purpose in the present immediacy of a kingdom not of this world. Love neither rules, nor is it unmoved; also it is a little oblivious as to morals. It does not look to the future; for it finds its own reward in the immediate present.[42]

Whitehead's refusal to accept imperial ruler as a metaphor for God found expression in *Modes of Thought* as well. The ancient world borrowed characteristics from "touchy, vain, imperious tyrants" to describe God. This history still influences contemporary civilized religion to envision gods as dictators. As Whitehead observed, only in Buddhism and the Christian gospels are there scattered repudiations of this image of divinity.[43]

John B. Cobb Jr. and David Ray Griffin have expanded the list of metaphors that are unacceptable in a Whiteheadian conception of God to include five: God as cosmic moralist, God as the unchanging and passionless absolute, God as controlling power, God as sanctioner of the status quo, God as male.[44] Clearly, the sentiments of feminists and Whiteheadians are similar in their rejection of traditional theism and in their effort to discover metaphors for God that are more inclusive of diverse experience.

In the theological and metaphysical concepts, Whiteheadians envision new paradigms of power and love that are attractive to feminists and compatible with feminist thinking. In Plato's writing, Whitehead found what he proclaimed to be one of the greatest intellectual discoveries in the history of religion—"that the divine element in the world is to be conceived as a persuasive agency and not as a coercive agency."[45] Along with the insights of Charles Hartshorne, Whitehead's concept of persuasion (in contrast to coercion) has formed the basis for development of both divine and social images of power. John B. Cobb Jr. describes this divine persuasive power as the means of exercising power over the powerful. Divine persuasion "depends rather on relations of respect, concern, and love, and the vision of a better future" and "is a balance between urging toward the good and maximizing the power—therefore the freedom—of the one whom God seeks to persuade."[46]

Bernard Loomer formulated an idea of relational power based on the process-relational view of reality and in contrast to a linear or unilateral conception of power. Linear power is unidirectional power that is intended to produce an effect in another by virtue of a capacity to "influence, guide, adjust, manipulate, shape, control, or transform the human or natural environment in order to advance one's purposes."[47] Relational power, on the other hand, is grounded in mutuality. It assumes the capacity to influence others and to be influenced by others. Thus, if one is powerful, one is able to include in oneself feelings and values of others without passivity or loss of identity. Relational power is active openness. "Our openness to be influenced by another, without losing our identity or sense of self-dependence, is not only an acknowledgement and affirmation of the other as an end rather than a means to an end. It is also a measure of our own strength and size, even and especially when this influence of the other helps to effect a creative transformation of ourselves and our world."[48] Although these formulations of divine persuasive power and relational power are not without problems for some feminists, they do represent alternatives to coercive, hierarchical power patterns and are suggestive of feminist reformulations of power in the context of mutuality. As one example, Rita Nakashima Brock has made use of Loomer's understanding of relational power in her construction of a theology of erotic power.[49] Erotic power is one of the defining characteristics of Christa/Community, Brock's reformulation of Christology in relational terms.[50]

William J. Hill has specifically addressed the topic of divine love in the Whiteheadian conceptuality. In his analysis, he found in Whitehead a concept of divine love that lies in contrast to New Testament *agape* and medieval *amicitia* and that identifies with Platonic *eros*. In *Adventures of Ideas*, what Whitehead calls the primordial nature of God, the abstract and eternal aspect of God's nature that envisions ideals and beckons us toward our potentials, is referred to as Eros. The love implied by *eros* relates to the divine envisioning of possibilities for fulfillment in each occasion. Hill has suggested three structural points in Whitehead's philosophy that support this interpretation of divine love. First, God's relation to the world is neither strictly free nor creative, because both God and the world are necessary. Second, God's motive with respect to loving the world is God's own satisfaction. Third, values realized in the world immediately perish and are preserved in God in such a way that they fund God's own creative becoming. Hill has also suggested that the strength of this view of love is God's involvement in the suffering of the world.[51]

Hill has certainly selected the relevant features of Whitehead's concept of God that support the concept of divine *eros*; however, Hill's interpretation tends to diminish the rich vision intended by Whitehead. Whitehead's point was certainly that God is relational, but if God's power is persuasive, then God's loving relating is directed toward maximal freedom and creativity for the world. Such love can only be directed toward entities that are other centers of power. In its immanence, this love lures toward novelty and participates in every creative moment. In the second and third points, Hill has shifted the discussion to what Whitehead calls the consequent nature of God, the relative and everlasting pole of God's nature that appreciates and receives all experiences; and at this point, Hill clearly deviates from an application of *eros* to the primordial nature of God. This is not entirely objectionable, because it is the genius of Whitehead's metaphysics that God and the world are truly in relation such that "it is as true to say that God creates the World, as that the World creates God."[52] If God and the world are related, then, within the Whiteheadian conceptuality, it must be expected that God will affect the world and that the world will affect God—that the world will receive from God and that God will receive from the world.

Process theologian Daniel Day Williams may provide feminists with a theological resource for construction of this view of God. Williams believed that the mutuality between God and humans is expressed in love, which is the meaning of the *imago Dei*. God and humans experience mutual love as cocreators, both taking responsibility for creation. As lovers, God and humans in community are mutually responsive. This love defines power as persuasive; power is expressive of love and nurtures the freedom of the other. It is love that affirms selfhood in oneself and the other.[53]

From a feminist perspective, why not affirm this mutuality of relationship and re-vision the divine *eros*? The redefinition of *eros* will then refer to an aim toward mutual satisfaction. Thus, God lures the world toward satisfaction, and the world contributes to God's satisfaction. God's appreciation for the world becomes an investment of godself in its values and suffering, for God is willing to receive both into godself. *Eros*, then, may be understood as creative, responsive, and empathetic. If God's love is named *eros* by this definition, then the transformative power of God's love as a paradigm for human loving feeds a feminist vision of mutuality. Why not revive the divine *eros* in feminist theism? Sallie McFague answers my question by creating exactly this metaphorical revival in *Models of God: Theology for an Ecological, Nuclear Age*.[54] The connection of God and *eros* appears most directly in her metaphor of God as Lover but also in her image of the world as God's body. Rita Nakashima Brock, too, revives this connection of God and *eros*. Brock describes God/dess as Heart, the present divine erotic power.[55]

JOINING VOICES

My feminist cosmology joins voices from feminist and Whiteheadian theorists in the principles described above and their application. To summarize, there are several major points at which feminists make contact with Whitehead's philosophy or regarding which feminists and Whiteheadians have a common concern.

1. Feminists find in Whitehead's philosophy a satisfying conceptuality for interpreting experience.
2. Feminists identify with Whitehead's emphasis on experience as the basis for metaphysics.
3. Feminists can appreciate Whitehead's understanding of the perspectival intellect that suggests a "logic" or reasoning process based on importance.
4. Feminists and Whiteheadians affirm the essential connection between intellect and experience.
5. Feminists can affirm the Whiteheadian attempt to overcome dualisms.
6. Whiteheadians and feminists value change, which has significance for describing a dynamic universe and which is the basis of hope for feminist movement.
7. The doctrine of internal relations may suggest a concept and fruitful metaphors for feminist expression of relationality.
8. Feminism and Whiteheadian philosophy are characterized by an emphasis on the value of nature.
9. Feminists can point to the Whiteheadian conception of God as an alternative to classical theism.

These compatibilities suggest that feminists may find it useful to interact with Whiteheadian thought in the re-vision of interrelatedness. Embracing this process of encounter itself embodies the potential for emergence of a process feminist theory of relations.

Another way to summarize the connection of Whiteheadian and feminist perspectives is to say that these perspectives have in common a critical response to the modern worldview and they propose similar alternatives. Catherine Keller, a Whiteheadian feminist, has described this movement toward the postmodern:

We may confidently assert that the desiderata of a postmodern world . . . bear an intimate resemblance to the worldview emerging as intrinsic to feminist thought and praxis. Both are generating creative alternatives to the traditional (and quintessentially modern) dualisms of body and mind, matter and spirit, self and other, world and deity. Both propose value structures and social institutions based on individuation within a matrix of interdependence, and both hope thus to obliterate relations of dominance and submission. Both generate an organic and interconnected worldsense to replace the depersonalizing individualism perpetrated by a machine economy.[56]

These characteristics of the postmodern worldview are shared by Whitehead. The compatibility of feminism and Whiteheadian thought characterize both as postmodern, and much of the similarity in feminism and Whiteheadian philosophy is a critical and creative response to the modern worldview.

My constructive project here involves assessing not only the complementarity of Whitehead's philosophy and feminism but also assessing the significance of the differences. The extensive overlap in Whiteheadian and feminist concerns does not preclude important differences. Some of these differences fund the thesis that Whitehead may be useful to feminists constructing a theory of relations, because Whitehead's unique ideas have insights to offer feminism. There are points of difference between feminism and Whitehead, however, where feminists will need to be discerning about reliance on Whitehead's philosophy. In spite of Whitehead's sympathy for women's issues and the compatibility of Whiteheadian thought and feminism, it is important to remember Mary Daly's warning that feminists should beware of prefabricated theory. Whitehead's philosophy of organism must also be examined for the patriarchal and hierarchical elements that it contains. There are points at which Whitehead's thought must be revised and Whitehead's interpreters challenged in light of women's experience. Assessing the differences creatively and critically is the task of the remaining chapters of this manuscript.

Although Whiteheadian thought is not free of patriarchal and hierarchical elements, it is not a closed system. As feminist ideas and experiences are applied to process philosophy, it may be transformed and revised more appropriately to reflect the widest possible range of experience. I propose that Whitehead's organic philosophy is remarkably helpful for constructing a feminist theory of relations, and I note that feminists are making a contribution to process thought by constructing a postpatriarchal, process-relational philosophy.

NOTES

1. Margaret A. Farley, *Personal Commitments: Beginning, Keeping, Changing* (San Francisco: Harper & Row, 1986).
2. Charlene Spretnak, *The Spiritual Dimension of Green Politics* (Santa Fe, N. Mex: Bear & Company, 1986).
3. Valerie C. Saiving, "Androgynous Life: A Feminist Appropriation of Process Thought" (The Harvard University Dudelian Lecture), in *Feminism and Process Thought: The Harvard Divinity School/Claremont Center for Process Studies Symposium Papers*, ed. Sheila Greeve Davaney (New York and Toronto: Edwin Mellen Press, 1981), 12–13.
4. Penelope Washbourn, "The Dynamics of Female Experience: Process Models and Human Values," in *Feminism and Process Thought: The Harvard Divinity School/Claremont Center for Process Studies Symposium Papers*, ed. Sheila Greeve Davaney (New York and Toronto: Edwin Mellen Press, 1981), 83.
5. Marjorie Suchocki, "Openness and Mutuality in Process Thought and Feminist Action," in *Feminism and Process Thought: The Harvard Divinity School/ Claremont Center for Process Studies Symposium Papers*, ed. Sheila Greeve Davaney (New York and Toronto: Edwin Mellen Press, 1981), 62–63.
6. Mary Daly, *Beyond God the Father: Toward a Philosophy of Women's Liberation* (Boston: Beacon Press, 1973), 189.
7. Saiving, "Androgynous Life," 13. Saiving's reference is to Alfred North Whitehead, *Process and Reality: Corrected Edition*, eds. David Ray Griffin and Donald W. Sherburne (New York: Free Press, 1978), 16, 160.
8. Alfred North Whitehead, *Modes of Thought* (New York: Macmillan Company, 1938), 4.
9. Ibid., 7–8.
10. Alfred North Whitehead, *Adventures of Ideas* (New York: Free Press, 1967), 226.
11. Saiving, "Androgynous Life," 12.
12. Whitehead, *Process and Reality*, 338.
13. Ibid., 337.
14. Whitehead, *Modes of Thought*, 5.
15. Ibid., 9.
16. Ibid., 11.
17. Sallie McFague, *Metaphorical Theology: Models of God in Religious Language* (Philadelphia: Fortress Press, 1982), 152.
18. Letty M. Russell, *Human Liberation in a Feminist Perspective—A Theology* (Philadelphia: Westminster Press, 1974), 55.
19. Patricia Hill Collins, *Black Feminist Thought: Knowledge, Consciousness, and the Politics of Empowerment* (New York: Routledge, 1990), 28–29.
20. McFague, *Metaphorical Theology*, 103.
21. For a detailed discussion of the relationship of importance and activity, see Whitehead, *Modes of Thought*, 159–71.
22. Daly, *Beyond God the Father*, 189.
23. Dorothee Soelle with Shirley A. Cloyes, *To Work and to Love: A Theology of Creation* (Philadelphia: Fortress Press, 1984), 24.
24. John B. Cobb Jr., "The Intrapsychic Structure of Christian Existence," *Journal of the American Academy of Religion* 36 (December 1968): 330. See this article and "Strengthening the Spirit," *Union Seminary Quarterly Review* 30

(Winter–Summer 1975): 130–39 for a detailed Whiteheadian interpretation of persons as psychosomatic unities.
25. Whitehead, *Process and Reality*, 24.
26. Soelle, *To Work and to Love*, 25.
27. Whitehead, *Process and Reality*, 22.
28. Anne Wilson Schaef, *Women's Reality: An Emerging Female System in the White Male Society* (Minneapolis: Winston Press, 1981), 144.
29. Whitehead, *Process and Reality*, 22.
30. Ibid., 221.
31. Schaef, *Women's Reality*, 108.
32. Beverly Wildung Harrison, *Our Right to Choose: Toward a New Ethic of Abortion* (Boston: Beacon Press, 1983), 99–100.
33. Catherine Keller, *From a Broken Web: Separation, Sexism, and Self* (Boston: Beacon Press, 1986). See especially chapter 1 in which Keller defines the separate self and the soluble self and pages 182–88 in which Keller uses Whitehead's concept of internal relations to construct a relational view of selfhood.
34. See, for example, Mary Daly, *Pure Lust: Elemental Feminist Philosophy* (Boston: Beacon Press, 1984), ix.
35. Alice Walker, *The Color Purple* (New York: Washington Square Press; Pocket Books, 1982), 178.
36. Susan Griffin, *Woman and Nature: The Roaring Inside Her* (New York: Harper & Row; Colophon Books, 1978), 219.
37. Sharon Doubiago, "Mama Coyote Talks to the Boys," in *Healing the Wounds: The Promise of Ecofeminism*, ed. Judith Plant (Philadelphia: New Society Publishers, 1989), 43.
38. Judith Plant, ed., *Healing the Wounds: The Promise of Ecofeminism* (Philadelphia: New Society Publishers, 1989), 255.
39. Whitehead, *Modes of Thought*, 38.
40. Whitehead, *Adventures of Ideas*, 205.
41. Whitehead, *Process and Reality*, 107.
42. Ibid., 343.
43. Whitehead, *Modes of Thought*, 68.
44. John B. Cobb Jr. and David Ray Griffin, *Process Theology: An Introductory Exposition* (Philadelphia: Westminster Press, 1969), 8–10.
45. Whitehead, *Adventures of Ideas*, 166.
46. John B. Cobb Jr., *God and the World* (Philadelphia: Westminster Press, 1969), 90.
47. Bernard Loomer, "Two Conceptions of Power," *Process Studies* 6 no. 1 (Spring 1976): 8.
48. Ibid., 18.
49. Rita Nakashima Brock, "Power, Peace, and the Possibility of Survival," in *God and Global Justice: Religion and Poverty in an Unequal World*, ed. Frederick Ferré and Rita H. Mataragnon (New York: Paragon House; New Era Book, 1985), 17–35.
50. Rita Nakashima Brock, *Journeys by Heart: A Christology of Erotic Power* (New York: Crossroad, 1988).
51. William J. Hill, "Two Gods of Love: Aquinas and Whitehead," *Listening* 14 no. 3 (Fall 1979): 258–59.
52. Whitehead, *Process and Reality*, 348.
53. Daniel Day Williams, *The Spirit and the Forms of Love* (Washington, D.C.: University Press of America, 1981), 134–37. The original publication is

The Spirit and the Forms of Love (New York: Harper & Row, 1968), 134–37.

54. Sallie McFague, *Models of God: Theology for an Ecological, Nuclear Age* (Philadelphia: Fortress Press, 1987).

55. Brock, *Journeys by Heart*, 46.

56. Catherine Keller, "Toward a Postpatriarchal Postmodernity," in *Spirituality and Society: Postmodern Visions*, ed. David Ray Griffin (Albany: State University of New York Press, 1988), 63–64.

T h r e e

RELATING TO NATURE

FEMINIST LITERATURE OF VARIOUS types expresses a commitment to the idea that humans (women, at least) are connected to nature. The relationship of humans and nature is depicted as intimate, nondualistic kinship. This portrayal contrasts sharply with dualistic, hierarchical, and anthropocentric perspectives that describe the relationship as a rather remote biological connection and emphasize the distance between humans and nature by concentrating on the superiority and complexity of humans. Because much scholarship has proliferated these views of nature, the burden of proof has fallen to women and others sympathetic with an ecological perspective to demonstrate the close continuity of humans and nature, the interdependence of humans and nature, and the interplay of the intrinsic and instrumental values of both humans and nature. This task crosses disciplines and calls on the expertise of physicists, biochemists, biologists, animal behaviorists, physical anthropologists, environmentalists, ecologists, philosophers, theologians, ethicists, poets, and novelists.

UTOPIA

Feminist novelists and poets are among the women who are exploring alternative perspectives on the relationship of humans and nature. Feminist utopian literature is one literary genre in which women's intuitions and valuations concerning nature are developed with few patriarchal inhibitions and accusations of sentimentality. By way of introduction to a feminist perspective on nature, we can look toward this literature as an imaginative expression of feminist revisions. *Wanderground: Stories of the Hill Women*, by Sally Miller Gearhart, is a feminist utopian literary vehicle for exploring a feminist nature-encompassing and nature-valuing reality.[1]

Gearhart's stories have coherence in the common imaginative history of each. The stories chronicle the adventures of women who have escaped from the City where they were subject to rape, murder, assault, and control by men. Violence toward women was extreme (although not unrealistic, if compared with actual statistics on violence toward women), and it resulted in an "underground railroad" of women escaping from the City to the wilderness hills, mountains, and deserts. In the wilderness, women created a new life for themselves in relationship with nature. These outlaw women represented to each other and to the gentles (men to whom outlaw women let themselves be known) hope for the earth's survival.[2]

One notable characteristic of the relationship between the outlaw women and nature is that they have the capacity for direct communication. Communication is possible through touch, spoken words, and shortstretch (a form of mindstretch, a nonverbal sort of telepathic or interpsychic communication). I note three vignettes as examples. In the first, the outlaw woman Alaka communicates by touch with the fish who swim underwater around her. The touch of woman and fish is described as a touch of mutual greeting.[3] In the second, Fora travels with her companion Lady to the deep cella, a chamber deep in the earth where women go for the ritual of impregnation. Fora's companion Lady is a sparrow who shares her anxiety and excitement and who communicates with Fora by sending messages through mindstretch.[4] Mutual "feeling" occurs between women and nature. In the third vignette, Alaka explores the land on her journey and the land responds in like manner.

> By swift montage she listened to and felt one at a time, every thing, every oxygen-breathing thing, every other-breathing thing, every non-breathing thing. They felt her attention and told her all was well.[5]

Communication between nature and women is not limited to living animals. It extends to the most fundamental elements in nature. On Alaka's journey, she speaks aloud with a rockbound pool whom she addresses as "Earthsister." The brief response of the pool surrounds her. About communication with the pool, we are told: "Alaka knew better than to stand in converse with so fundamental a substance. Such elements were to be moved with and felt into but never accosted or confronted."[6] In another case of communication with elemental nature, Diana petitions a cirrus cloud for assistance in an erotic, mystical ritual with the full moon. The cloud responds:

> She had to listen with her unintentional ear, give to the cloud only secondary or peripheral attention, and in fact pretend no attention at all to the cloud. When she did that, there was the cloud's gentle whispering at the back door of her mind. Diana laughed. It was not easy to speak so indirectly and the conversation was more a line than the usual seeping, but they understood each other.[7]

These two conversations with elemental nature have the character of reverence, mystery, and awe. The women relate to elemental nature as religious persons approaching a deity.

The purpose of communication with nature generally concerns women's interdependence with nature. The ecosystem of the Wanderground is an intimate interconnection. The relationship of women and nature is one of mutual assistance. For example, at the end of Alaka's long underwater swim through the rockbound pool, a large tree root assists her from the water. She mindstretches her thanks to the tree, which responds, "Again if you need me."[8] Another story tells of a tree expressing gratitude to a hill woman for removing a trap from its trunk because it wanted no part in injuring an animal. In other instances, women thank nature for food and resources prior to taking or using them.

Nature is a source of knowledge and strength for the women. On one hand, the mixture of blood and earth have healing power. Earthtouch provides protection and emotional grounding. Earthblood is a source of healing. On the other hand, the collective knowledge and history of women requires a relationship with animals. Cats are essential for remembering the history of women's oppression in the City, because cats recall history better than women. Without dichotomizing nature and culture, women are aware of their dependence on nature, even for historical memory.

The mutuality of the outlaw women and nature was not something that women brought with them from the City. The capacity to communicate with nature, to accept the assistance of nature, and to respond similarly had to be learned. The emergence of these capacities in relationship with nature (including women's increasing physical and psychic skills in their own bodies) was a matter of "learning to listen to what the land wants you to do."[9]

WOMEN AND NATURE

What *Wanderground* expresses well is that women sense and desire a genuine connection with nature—real communion, feeling, touching, and relationship with oxygen-breathing, other-breathing, and nonbreathing things. This sense of connectedness with nature means that women know what Alice Walker says through Shug in *The Color Purple*, "I knew that if I cut a tree my arm would bleed,"[10] and what Joanna Macy means by an ecological sense of selfhood, "I am part of the rainforest protecting myself."[11] This ecological sense of the shared connections and destinies of humans and nature resounds in the Native American spirituality expressed in the writings of Paula Gunn Allen, Dhyani Ywahoo, and Carol Lee Sanchez.

There is a paradox in the connection of women and nature. The conflicting views of patriarchy and feminism create some confusion due to the fact that each connects women to nature but with radically different consequences for our evaluation of women and nature. Many feminists see women in a positive relationship with nature, a kinship involving interdependence and mutual caretaking. On the other hand, the historical, patriarchal association of women and nature has been negative, because women and nature are connected by virtue of their inferiority. This patriarchal view results in the oppression of women and the destruction of nature.

Carolyn Merchant has analyzed the historical association of women and nature in light of two predominant female images of nature. The first image was that of nature as nurturing mother. In sixteenth-century Europe, the image of the earth as nurturing mother was part of an organic view of reality. In this view, nature met human needs as a good mother beneficently meets the needs of her children. The second image identified nature with the wild, uncontrollable female. This opposing image described the nature of storms, disaster, and chaos. The Scientific Revolution introduced a mechanistic view of the universe which resulted in a shift away from the image of nature as nurturing mother. The machine entered history as the controlling imagery and with it mastery over nature as wild and uncontrollable female became ingrained in the modern worldview. This imagery for nature served the purposes of commercialism and industrialism by using female metaphors to permit exploitation and manipulation of nature. One can justify exploitative, dominating behavior toward nature as wild woman but not toward the nurturing mother.[12] Exploitation of women and nature were connected. This is the negative side of the association of women and nature.

Vandana Shiva, an ecofeminist scientist and activist in India, has observed a shift in female and nature imagery that has led to the exploitation of women and nature in the sphere of economic development. Women and nature were once associated with the Hindu feminine principle and its qualities of activity, productivity, and creativity. These admirable qualities were appropriated by men to characterize what is male. Women and nature (as the "other") were reduced to passive resources for the furtherance of "maldevelopment" of male-defined economic progress.[13] When identification of women and nature is positive, women and nature are viewed as nurturers, creators, and sustainers of life. What Shiva has argued, on the other hand, is that colonialism, modern economics, and development exemplify the negative side of the association of women and nature, because both resources are exploited and victimized in the social and ecological consequences of economic development.

Susan Griffin has realized, with other feminist scholars, that the connection of women and nature is not the entire issue. The issue also involves the problem of male alienation from nature and women.

> He says that woman speaks with nature. That she hears voices from under the earth. That wind blows in her ears and trees whisper to her. That the dead sing through her mouth and the cries of infants are clear to her. But for him this dialogue is over. He says he is not part of this world, that he was set on this world as a stranger. He sets himself apart from woman and nature.[14]

The problem is not so much the distinction between men and women or men and nature or the connection between women and nature. Such distinctions enhance diversity, potentiality, and creative contrast. The problem is one of alienation, separation, and absolute individuality.

Delores Williams's *Sisters in the Wilderness* suggests a cautionary note regarding male alienation from nature and female connection with nature. Using the biblical accounts of Hagar, the Egyptian slave of Sarah, and U.S. African-American history, Williams gives careful attention to the role of wilderness (or nature) as intellectual, social, and political symbol in the black community. Wilderness, on one hand, represents danger, vulnerability, isolation, and trouble and, on the other hand, God's personal direction, support, and assistance in survival.[15] For the slave, wilderness signified religious experience, so that both intense spiritual struggles and strengthened religious life carried positive connotations.[16] After emancipation, wilderness was an ambivalent symbol meaning both a sacred place for encounter with God and a hostile and insecure place where families attempted to make a living.[17] Out of this history, Williams suggests that "in black theology today, the wilderness experience is a more appropriate name than the black experience to describe African-American existence in North America."[18] Wilderness experience describes the inclusive experience of black community, male and female.[19]

DUALISM

Feminist claims that men are alienated from women and nature suggest that dualistic patterns of thinking are a root cause. African-American scholar Patricia Hill Collins explains well how thinking in dichotomized pairs of opposites leads to subordination. What I refer to as dualism, Collins refers to as either/or dichotomous thinking. Either/or dichotomous thinking categorizes things, persons, and ideas on the basis of their differences. Counterparts give each other meaning but at the cost of opposition and objectification. Because domination enforces objectification and because there is rarely equality in oppositional pairs, subordination is the means of resolving tension between opposites such as mind/body or culture/nature. Subsequently, we draw conclusions that mind is superior to body, and culture is superior to nature.[20]

Alienation of men from women and nature is based on the dualism of culture and nature and on the dualism of spirit and matter. These two dualistic pairs are repeatedly cited in feminist literature as the source of human and environmental injustice. Although it is not necessary that dualism create alienation, the culture/nature dichotomy and the spirit/matter dichotomy substantially support the valuation of men over women and nature and ultimately endorse the exploitation of women and nature.

Lynn White first published what women have claimed in this regard in his article on the Christian origins of the ecological crisis.

> Especially in its Western form, Christianity is the most anthropocentric religion the world has seen. . . . Man shares, in great measure, God's transcendence of nature. Christianity, in absolute contrast to ancient paganism and Asia's religions (except, perhaps, Zoroastrianism), not only established a dualism of man and nature but also insisted that it is God's will that man exploit nature for his proper ends.[21]

How is it that this dualism has led to exploitation? How have women and nature shared the role of victimization? Briefly, I shall summarize a feminist argument that the association of men with culture and spirit in tandem with the coidentity of women and nature logically results in the minimization of the intrinsic value assigned to women and nature and in the objectification of women and nature as resources for exploitation.

Susan Griffin's article "Split Culture" argues that we live in a delusion that divides us from the earth, fellow creatures, and part of our own being (our experience and our bodies). This delusion includes alienation of our sexuality into male and female poles. These divisions are decided by an overarching separation between nature and that which is superior to nature.[22] Religion has supported this alienating worldview by appeal to the separation of pure spirit and corrupt matter (that is, God and angels in contrast to earthly things) and the metaphorical extension of this separation to the earthly sphere (so that humans are superior to animals, males to females, white males to others).[23] The authority of scripture and of priests supports this duality, and we are told to distrust our own minds, feelings, and senses in the experience of a different reality. Science has reinforced the alienation in ways similar to religion by convincing us to defer to the authority of the scientist and so-called objective truth. "In both systems, not only are we alienated from a world that is described as deceiving us; we are also alienated from our own capacity to see and hear, to taste and touch, to know and describe our own experience."[24]

The collusion of religion and science convinces us that we should control nature. The delusion is that we should distrust the natural order and trust the cultural order (an order that we have created, by and large, through religion and science). By using culture to control nature, we create an illusion of safety that masks our self-deception. Our self-deception is that we are not a part of the natural order that we attempt to control, manipulate, and exploit. Within ourselves, the deception fragments us into culture and nature, a fragmentation that leads to the valuation of intelligence over the physical body and senses.[25] Parts of nature and symbols of nature (such as women) suffer the control of "supernatural" culture. Psychologically speaking, the attempt to control is intensified by the anxiety and fear produced in the face of cultural delusion.

> The mind that invents a delusion of power over Nature in order to feel safe is afraid of fear itself. And the more this mind learns to rely on delusion, the less tolerance this mind has for any betrayal of that delusion. For we must remember that this mind has denied that it itself is a thing of Nature. It has begun to identify not only its own survival, but its own existence with culture. The mind believes that it exists because what it thinks is true. Therefore, to contradict delusion is to threaten the mind's very existence. And the ideas, words, numbers, concepts have become more real to this mind than material reality.[26]

In a sense, the delusion feeds itself and becomes ever more controlling. The dualisms of culture/nature and spirit/matter and the superior valuation of culture and spirit are rarely analyzed as the source of the alienation and fear, so the delusion and anxiety are only heightened.

DOMINATION AND HIERARCHY

Starhawk calls the worldview that shapes our consciousness "estrangement." It is the same worldview that Susan Griffin has described as separating humans from nature, other humans, and their own bodies and senses. Finally, this worldview is atomistic and sees all things as separate and isolated. The components of this atomistic world are seen as nonliving objects. With lifeless objects, the only relationship possible is one of manipulation and domination.[27]

Alienation or estrangement entails power relationships involving domination and hierarchy. Hierarchy may be defined as a systematized order that assigns on a continuum or to dichotomized pairs either superior value and authority (supremacy) or inferior value and authority (subordination) to its members. In this brief definition, dualism (either/or dichotomized thinking) is associated with hierarchy. Patricia Hill Collins's discussion of dichotomous thinking leads her to this conclusion:

> The foundations of a complex social hierarchy become grounded in the interwoven concepts of either/or dichotomous thinking, oppositional differences, and objectification. With domination based on difference forming an essential underpinning for this entire system of thought, these concepts invariably imply relationships of superiority and inferiority, hierarchical bonds that mesh with political economies of race, gender, and class oppression.[28]

Karen Warren also argues that there is a connection between value-hierarchical thinking and value-dualisms. Although Warren is not convinced that hierarchy is problematic in itself, she contends that when hierarchy is coupled with a logic of domination, we create an oppressive conceptual system that creates and maintains subordination of those whose inferiority is established by virtue of difference from the dominant group.[29]

The foundational article "Is Female to Male as Nature Is to Culture?" by Sherry Ortner explains how a dualistic view of male/female and culture/nature relies on close association of women and nature to support patriarchal hierarchy. Ortner's thesis is that "culture (still equated relatively unambiguously with men) recognizes that women are active participants in its special processes, but at the same time sees them as being more rooted in, or having more direct affinity with, nature."[30] In the nature/culture split, women are intermediaries. Women are seen as closer to nature because they reproduce the species. Hence, women's social role is defined in terms of female reproductive capacities. This social definition of women concretizes woman's identification with nature and alienates woman from culture as a sort of cultural pollutant. This connection of women and nature, in their common alienation from culture, means that the male/female relationship of hierarchy and domination cannot be overcome apart from the similar rejection of the human/nature hierarchy.

Beginning with Ortner's article, Rosemary Ruether furthers the argument that the culture/nature and spirit/matter dualisms have developed historically as a rationalization for domination and hierarchy. Ruether starts her historical analysis by examining male puberty rites and their psychological implications. Women's role was established through woman's identification with childbearing, childrearing, and domestic responsibility. Confining women to the domestic sphere placed a limitation on the social mobility of women. This view of women, together with the success of men in hunting and warfare, established men as the ones who define culture. Psychologically speaking, men are then socialized through separation from the domestic sphere of women. Male socialization is a process that involves alienation from women and devaluation of women. Male puberty rites reflect this alienation and devaluation by enacting a mythic overthrow of an original matriarchy. Male transcendence of matriarchy, symbolized in the male puberty rites, creates a cultural paradigm. This myth is perpetuated through the role of women. Women's energies are constrained by their responsibility for routine domestic and economic chores, whereas men, unencumbered by similar tedious tasks, are free to exercise control over cultural affairs. Women are defined culturally as objects and symbolize male control over matter.[31] Male puberty rites are a cultural symbol, suggesting how the culture/nature and spirit/matter dichotomies participate in the establishment of a male-dominated hierarchy.

The symbols of both woman and nature have ambivalent interpretations.

Woman has symbolized the devalued, lower parts of the self, as well as the divine source of life. Nature has symbolized both that which is to be controlled and dominated and that which is divine cosmic order.[32] Ruether describes how specific historical, ideological developments in the Western world have led to the prominence of inferior imagery for women and nature and the obscuring of divine imagery for women and nature.

Ruether finds one reason for the prominence of inferior imagery for women and nature in Greek thought, where the human mind was raised to the level of transcendent deity, and the visible world and the body were objectified. This created a dualism of mind and matter or body, which treated the body or matter as inferior to the mind. The Greek view was that transcendent mind is engaged in a struggle to subdue lower matter. For both Aristotle and Plato, women symbolized lower matter, which needed to be controlled by the mind. This Greek worldview not only established a cosmic hierarchy—from the highest forms, God and spiritual creatures, to man and woman, and the lower creatures—but it also created a system of domination and a doctrine of salvation that required alienation from the body and matter.

The hierarchy of spirit to physical nature as male to female is made explicit. The chain of being, God-spirits-male-female-nonhuman nature-matter, is at the same time the chain of command. The direction of salvation follows the trajectory of alienation of mind from its own physical support system, objectified as body and matter.[33]

Ruether continues by describing how spirituality in the Greco-Roman world rendered women and the body (and, therefore, nature) inferior. The alienation of transcendent mind from objectified matter resulted in a world-fleeing spirituality. To attain immortality, the spirit had to separate itself from the world of matter. Women represented the sexual bearing of life and consequently symbolized death and mortality. The image of male spirit transcending mortality symbolized salvation. This meant that for a woman to attain salvation or immortality, she had to fragment herself from her sexual and maternal identity.[34] Spirit and mind could commune with the divine sphere. Body and nature were severed from any kind of association with the divine.

Ruether notes how Christianity was affected by the influence of Greek and Roman thought when orthodox Christianity adopted a similar worldview. Asceticism, which alienated women from their own bodies, was a way by which women could attain spiritual equality with men. The ascetic path for women, however, was repressed as patriarchy was accepted as the normative order. With the rise of patriarchal imagery that eliminated the ascetic option for women, women could only attain spiritual equality in heaven. This postponed equality was attained by subjugation to patriarchal power in both church and society.[35] Christianity contributed to the further estrangement of women from spirit.

Finally, Ruether observes that the Renaissance and the Scientific Revolution clearly extended the idea of the superiority of mind over nature. The scientific method viewed man the knower as outside the object of observation and experimentation. Mind was abstracted from the object of knowledge. This ideological transcendence of the male mind over nature was accompanied by the rise of a mechanistic model of the cosmos and a resulting increase in manipulation of nature.[36] The mechanistic model objectified nature, and the transcendent mind dominated and attempted to control this object.

The historical legacy outlined by Ruether is an inheritance of modern technological, industrial society. Margo Adair and Sharon Howell describe how power relationships victimizing women and nature sustain industrial society. Industrial society depends on the domination of both nature and persons. The desire for wealth is a motivation for exploitation of nature and for maintaining a hierarchical order. Nature provides the resources for accumulating wealth, although some people are devalued and subjugated in order that others may become wealthy.[37] How is this possible? Subjugated persons have internalized a patriarchal view of humans and nature, so that it requires less and less power to control and dominate people and nature. Part of the internalization of patriarchy-hierarchy is learning to trust technology instead of the processes in nature. Internalization of a patriarchal worldview subdues impulses to resist exploitation of nature and people.[38]

Rachel Carson, in *Silent Spring*, alerts us that trust in technology is misplaced. Carson's work exposes the deception in technology and suggests that there are ecological alternatives. She concludes *Silent Spring* with a startling (for the 1960s) indictment of technology in arms against insects.

> The current vogue for poisons has failed utterly to take into account these most fundamental considerations. As crude a weapon as the cave man's club, the chemical barrage has been hurled against the fabric of life—a fabric on the one hand delicate and destructible, on the other miraculously tough and resilient, and capable of striking back in unexpected ways. These extraordinary capacities of life have been ignored by the practitioners of chemical control who have brought to their task no "high-minded orientation," no humility before the vast forces with which they tamper.
>
> The "control of nature" is a phrase conceived in arrogance, born of the Neanderthal age of biology and philosophy, when it was supposed that nature exists for the convenience of man. The concepts and practices of applied entomology for the most part date from that Stone Age of science. It is our alarming misfortune that so primitive a science has armed itself with the most modern and terrible weapons, and that in turning them against the insects it has also turned them against the earth.[39]

What Carson exposes is the illusion that one can control nature. This technique in relating to nature is barbaric and ignores the fact that nature is vulnerable to destruction *and* resilient enough to strike back at attempts to control. Control and hierarchical "power over" are primitive myths directing the human relationship with nature.

ECOFEMINISM

That the domination and exploitation of nature and women have the same origins and that a patriarchal hierarchy is the cultural context for such domination and exploitation reveal that the struggle for women's liberation is a struggle for environmental justice. Those who suffer hierarchical domination, even those who benefit marginally from control over nature, and women like Rachel Carson have launched severe criticisms of the worldview that supports domination and control. More important, women have joined the ecological movement to envision new principles and goals.

Ynestra King, an ecofeminist social ecologist, argues that the ecology movement needs feminism. It is true that feminism and ecology are complementary, but it is the ecology movement that needs to be persuaded that it has some investment in the issue of women's oppression. The ecology movement has special significance to women because of the oppression that women share with nature. Feminism has a distinct, indispensable contribution to make to ecology in the observation that misogyny and hatred of nature are connected. Ecofeminism, ecological feminism, recognizes that feminism and ecology require each other.[40]

The connection of feminism and ecology is the source of ecofeminist principles. Ynestra King summarizes four beliefs on which these principles are based. First, ecofeminists experience and take on the struggle of nature for life as their own struggle. This belief is based on the fact that the development of industrial culture in opposition to nature is related to the oppression of women and reinforces women's oppression. Second, nature is an interconnected web. Hierarchy is a cultural and social creation, which has been projected onto nature. All forms of domination are related to this cultural construct. Ecofeminism is antihierarchical. It is especially at this point that ecology and feminism work together.[41]

Ecofeminism also contributes an understanding of the connections between the domination of persons and the domination of nonhuman nature. Ecological science tells us that there is no hierarchy in nature itself, but rather a hierarchy in human society that is projected onto nature. Ecofeminism draws on feminist theory which asserts that the domination of woman was the original domination in human society, from which all other hierarchies—of rank, class, and political power—flow. Building on this unmasking of the ideology of natural hierarchy of persons, ecofeminism uses its ecological perspective to develop the position that there is no hierarchy in nature: among persons, between persons and the rest of the natural world, or among the many forms of nonhuman nature.[42]

Third, diversity is necessary to the ecosystem. Ecofeminism recognizes that diversity in nature, including diversity in the human population, promotes ecological health. Fourth, survival requires an understanding of the relationship of humans and nature. This means that we need to understand both nonhuman nature and our own bodies. It is important that we come to an understanding of nature that challenges the nature/culture dualism.[43]

King considers that there are three possible positions that feminism could take in response to the nature/culture dualism. Women could identify with culture and refuse the lower status connection with nature that patriarchy has assigned to women, or women could intensify their identification with nature in stark opposition with male identification with culture. King's ecofeminist position rejects these two alternatives for a third, suggesting that the connection of women and nature should not be rejected and also that women should not abnegate the role of creators of culture. The third option is that feminism should be employed with the creation of a new culture and politics toward the emergence of a free ecological society.[44]

ISSUES FOR A COSMOLOGY

The range and depth of feminist scholarship seeking connection between women and nature is impressive. Represented in the preceding discussion, feminists from multiple disciplines have raised three central questions and then constructed fresh ways of seeing women and nature. First, feminists have asked, What is the nature of alienation between humans and nature? Feminist utopias, feminist theology, and ecofeminist theory suggest that masculine, spiritualist worldviews separate humans and nature. In literary and theological imaginations, feminist responses argue for the mutuality and interconnections of women and nature. In exploring contemporary options for describing the relationship of women and nature, feminist theologians, historians of science, and anthropologists have well noted the ambiguity of the historical connection of women and nature—a connection that on one hand is valuable, sacred, and powerful and that on the other hand fuels control, exploitation, and degradation in different historical periods.

Second, feminists have asked, Is dualism an adequate framework for understanding reality? Overwhelmingly, feminists reject dualism that dichotomizes spirit and matter, culture and nature, humans and nature, mind and body, in oppositional thinking that entails established assumptions about the superiority or superordinate value of spirit, culture, humans, and intelligence. Not only is dualism an oversimplification of the nature of reality, but dualism further exacerbates injustice toward women and nature. For example, the interplay of nature-environment and culture-history is obscured or ignored by dualistic thinking that separates nature and culture. A summary critical definition of dualism, constructed from the preceding discussion of feminist perspectives on women and nature, might entail this composite of ideas: *Dualism categorizes reality in terms of perceived pairs of opposites—for example, spirit/matter, culture/nature, mind/body, God/world. Dualism assumes that dichotomized pairs are invitations to either/or thinking and decisions based upon presupposed assessments of superiority/inferiority, superordination/subordination, value/disvalue. Dualism tends to overlook the option of the value and connection (or even the experience and existence) of both poles of the dichotomized pair.*

Third, feminists have asked, Is hierarchy a necessary or actual state of affairs in nature? Scientists, including feminist scientists, have provided evidence that hierarchy is not present in nature. For example, Donna Haraway's survey of primate studies suggests that hierarchy has been projected onto nature by primatologists who have interpreted primate troop behavior on the model of dominance hierarchy. By the early 1960s, more comprehensive observations of troops' behaviors raised questions about the selective observations and classifications of male primate behaviors. More inclusive observations of males and females and of times of day and seasons provided data that fit a more ecological model of troop organization.[45] As another example, scholars criticize interpretations of cell biology that are hierarchical, describing DNA as the "controlling" molecule that determines RNA production and regulates cell proteins. Although cell biologists realize that the cell nucleus and cytoplasm are mutually influencing, control images and even male-female courting and marriage metaphors persist in the scientific literature. Alternate interpretations suggest that steady-state models of the cell are better interpretations.[46] Ecologists provide further models that reject hierarchy in nature. Feminists, whose fields are philosophy, religion, social sciences, and political sciences, provide other arguments that reject hierarchy as a thinly veiled justification for domination. Feminist thought resists or rejects hierarchy, and feminist studies, then, might construct this composite critical definition of "hierarchy": *Hierarchy is the pervasive rank ordering of existents in nature, such as the chain of being, God-angels-humans-animals-vegetation-inorganic matter. Hierarchy is rooted in cultural, sociohistorical, and often uncritical assumptions about value, complexity, and superiority measured with respect to human or abstract divine norms. Related to a logic of domination, hierarchy fuels racism, sexism, heterosexism, and other forms of oppression including exploitation of nature. Hierarchy can entail atomism or individualism, while overlooking interrelations.*

Hierarchy, as a social construct projected onto nature, is often confused with objective truth and mistakenly assumes ontological permanence.

A feminist cosmology that considers the relationships of women and nature (or humans and nature) must be indebted to these foundational criticisms of alienation, dualism, and hierarchy, but there are difficult questions that remain to be addressed. First, feminist theory so strongly emphasizes the connections of women and nature that we must further wrestle with the question, Where is the disconnection? Is it true that women's relationship with nature is utopian harmony? Is it the case that all women are connected with nature in a uniform way, or are there differences rooted in race and class (as Susan Thistlethwaite suggests in *Sex, Race, and God*[47])?

Second, given the ambiguous history of the analogy and association between women and nature, what are the consequences of a feminist cosmology that perpetuates the connection of women and nature? How can we avoid reformulations of the women and nature relationship without inadvertently extracting women from culture and, therefore, maintaining the culture/nature dualism? Do women have such a unique connection with nature that culture can never learn the language of communication with nature?

Finally, because feminist theory notes the connection between the domination of women and the domination of nature, do we tend too easily to assume that all forms of domination are identical? What does it mean for a feminist cosmology to explore the complex patterns of exploitation by gender, race, class, and in nature? Are we oversimplifying the identities of the exploited—generic woman and monolithic nature—and the variety of oppressions? How are these multiple oppressions connected?

CONTINUITY

The current question is, Can Whitehead's philosophy make a contribution to a feminist cosmology? If so, what does Whiteheadian thought have to offer? It is my contention that Whiteheadian thought is a valuable resource for ecofeminist scholarship and praxis. There is a basis for assuming the value of process philosophy for ecofeminism in the similarity of the two perspectives. Two common beliefs are foundational for process philosophy and for ecofeminism. The first is that there is continuity within nature. On this point, Whiteheadian thought may affirm continuity even more radically than most feminism, because the continuity extends his doctrine of internal relatedness to inorganic nature as well as organic nature. The second shared belief is that humans have a vital connection with nature, that all of nature is interconnected.

To be precise about Whitehead's commitment to the view that there is continuity within nature, we may cite his definition of living body, an expansion of his definition of human body or animal body.[48] The living body is "a region of nature which is itself the primary field of the expressions issuing from each of its parts."[49] This definition indicates that those entities that are centers of expression and feeling are alive. Whitehead very clearly applies this description to both animal and vegetable bodies and expressly indicates that the distinction between animals and vegetables is not a sharp distinction.[50]

Whitehead contends that precise classification of organic and inorganic entities in nature may be useful for scientific investigation, but it is dangerous for nature. Scientific classifications obscure the fact that "the different modes of natural existence shade off into each other."[51] If we consult *Process and Reality*, we may add further evidence that Whitehead does not see sharp distinctions in the continuum of nature. A basic point for Whitehead is that there is no distinct boundary between living organisms and the inorganic environment. His perspective is that the difference between organic and inorganic nature is one of degree. This does not mean that the difference is unimportant, but his commentary affirms the continuity of all nature.[52]

This very point is important for Whiteheadians Charles Birch and John Cobb's definition of life. Birch and Cobb raise the issue of boundaries between the animate and the inanimate in light of the ambiguity of life on the hypothetical boundaries.[53] Viruses are a particularly good example of creatures possessing properties of the living and the nonliving. Another example is cellular organelles, which reproduce but are incapable of life independent of the cell. Birch and Cobb affirm that there is a hierarchy of complexity from the virus to the organelle to the cell, but they do not imagine that there is a clear boundary between animate and inanimate entities in nature. The distinction between animate and inanimate nature is blurred.[54] This point is significant for the ecological model of reality that Birch and Cobb develop, because the model incorporates the view that every entity is internally related to its environment. Such a model is relevant to both the living and the nonliving.[55] Humans are no exception to the model. Humans are continuous with the rest of nature as an integral part of the natural process.[56]

In the previous chapter, I have mentioned another feature of Whitehead's philosophy that underscores the continuity of humans with nonhuman nature. That is the expansion of the definition of living person to include higher animals. Humans and animals are living persons characterized by a dominant occasion of experience that coordinates and unifies the activities of the plurality of occasions and enduring objects that form the person. For example, whether it is I or my cat, a dominant occasion coordinates the complex activity of eating. Recall how involved the process of eating really is—the smell of hot soup arouses the appetite, I rise to find the source of the smell and serve myself, my hands miraculously manipulate soup to mouth, and my body converts the food to forms usable for its maintenance. Compare this activity with the likelihood of the dinner table performing the same functions, and you will have a sense of the complex work of the dominant occasion to enable coordinated human or animal activity.

Personal order is the linear, serial, object-to-subject inheritance of the past in the present. Personal order in humans and nature is one component of what Whitehead calls "the doctrine of the immanence of the past energizing in the present."[57] The linear, one-dimensional character of personal inheritance in conjunction with a contribution from the multiplicity of the actual world is called the vector-structure of nature. This mode of personal inheritance has an analogy in physical nature where there is a multidimensional, geometrical order and transference.

> There is thus an analogy between the transference of energy from particular occasion to particular occasion in physical nature and the transference of affective tone, with its emotional energy, from one occasion to another in any human personality.[58]

There is an analogy, for example, in the personal inheritance that moves me from smelling food to appetite to acquiring food to tasting and the physical inheritance that moves water from liquid in the presence of heat to boiling water to steam. Even the human body interacts with its environment in this physical type of inheritance.

Within Whitehead's philosophy, continuity of nature is additionally confirmed by the pervasive subjectivity of experience in all entities. All entities are both subjects and objects, but it is on the basis of the subjectivity of all actual occasions that Whiteheadians argue that both organic and inorganic entities are experiencing creatures. Whitehead's doctrine of internal relations includes the fact that each concrescing occasion is a subject which takes account of previous occasions in the actual world in its self-creation. In *Adventures of Ideas*, Whitehead says that the experiencing subject has a "concern" (in the Quaker sense) for the objects in its experience.[59] Whether this "concern" is conscious or nonconscious, the basis of the subject's experience of other entities is emotional; that is, it involves a response to the object which is a feeling (or prehension) with an affective tone, which determines how the subject will constitute itself in relation to the felt object.[60] For example, if two friends visit a sushi bar and see the same raw fish dishes, one may feel revulsion and respond with nausea, while the other feels pleasure and responds with ravenous hunger. Based on the different affective tone (feeling) that each brings to the food, the friends constitute themselves differently in relation to the food. Because the basis of experience is emotional and because subjectivity is not restricted to conscious decision or knowledge, all organic and inorganic entities have subjectivity in common.

In an article on nonhuman experience, Susan Armstrong-Buck interprets recent primate studies in light of the Whiteheadian system. Her work advances Whitehead's observation that there is continuity between humans and nature with respect to perception. Armstrong-Buck cites studies of language-skilled primates who demonstrate a capacity for self-consciousness. These recent studies indicate that nonhuman animal self-consciousness is even closer to human self-consciousness than Whitehead realized.[61] This research corroborates Whitehead's system and advances his thought by demonstrating that the continuity between humans and nonhuman animals with respect to perception is greater than Whitehead anticipated.

GRADATIONS OF VALUE

The extraordinary emphasis on the similarity and connectedness of humans and nonhuman nature characterizes both feminist and Whiteheadian thought. This common theme is evidence that Whiteheadian philosophy may be useful in furthering the goals of a feminist cosmology. At this point, it becomes important to discuss a dimension of Whitehead's system that is subject to feminist criticism. Although ecofeminism is deliberately antihierarchical, citing ecologists who claim that there is no natural hierarchy, Whitehead retains the idea of hierarchy in nature. This is the point in Whitehead's thought at which the differences in degree between humans and nonhumans becomes important as a difference in quality.

The hierarchical relationship in nature sketched by Whitehead referred particularly to the notions of living body and dominant occasions of experience which have already been mentioned. The animal body may be considered from two perspectives. From one perspective, the animal body is one center of experience and a singular primary field of experience. From another perspective, the animal body is a multiplicity of centers of experience (for example, the heart or an arm). These various centers of experience are mutually expressive of themselves and, at the same time, mutually responsive to the expressions of other centers. Expression and feeling (reception of expressions) characterize all the bodily centers of experience individually and as a unity.[62] Animal body experience as a unity is a higher level experience than the experience of the individual experiential centers making up the body, because the whole is a complex unity of the coordinated feelings from the various experiences that make up the body. The subordinate centers are specialized and, therefore, limited in the types of emotional feelings that they can receive. Although the animal body is dominated by one or more centers of experience, this dominant center is subject to limitation by its reception of expressions from the body. The superiority of the dominant center of experience is not a matter of autonomy from the body; it is qualified by the interdependence of the dominant center with the other centers of bodily experience.

Vegetable bodies generally do not have a dominant center of experience. To describe the vegetable body, Whitehead uses the term "democracy" to indicate that the multiplicity of centers of experience making up the vegetable body are decisive for its definition. Although the animal body, as a feudal society, cannot fully function in the event of loss of the dominant occasion, its overlord, the vegetable body, may be divided into smaller derivative democracies with independent survival value.[63]

Here, as on most points, Whitehead's differentiation gives way to an emphasis on continuity. There are examples of vegetation exhibiting some sort of dominance in the whole body. Likewise, some animals exemplify democratic independence in their bodies. Ordinary vegetation and higher animals represent the extreme exemplifications of the vegetable democracy and the animal body on a continuum of life.[64]

Whitehead further delineates four types of aggregation of existents through consideration of their relative capacities in comparison to the human conceptual propensity for novelty arising from diverse expressive bodily centers and unexpressed possibilities. The lowest type of existent is the nonliving aggregation. There is virtually no individual expression in the parts of the aggregate, which is extremely limited in capacity to decide. The aggregate is governed by the "average"—"the average is always there, stifling individuality."[65] Expression of the average ensures the survival of the aggregrate according to the laws of nature.

The second type of existent is the democracy of the vegetable body. The parts of the vegetable body contribute purposeful influences to the whole, the aim of which is survival of the coordinated, organic individual and its expressiveness. The vegetable grade of existent is still expressive of the average, yet its coordinated complexity dominates the average. The expressiveness of the parts of the vegetative body are limited by the coordinated vegetable organism.[66] The vegetable body achieves a new level of existence, which exceeds that of the inorganic aggregate.

The third level existent is the animal body, which attains a higher grade of existence by virtue of the dominant occasion that is supported by its bodily parts. The dominant occasion makes it possible for the animal body to exceed the aim of survival in varying advanced degrees of purpose.[67]

The highest level is achieved in the level four existent, the human grade. The human grade existent exceeds the animal grade by the more sophisticated, complex capacities orchestrated by the dominant occasion. The human grade is characterized by greater consciousness, abstraction, purpose, and novelty. Morality and religion are possible in this highest grade of existence.[68]

These four types of aggregates are differentiated by their relative proportions of average expression and individual expression. The inorganic aggregate is largely capable of average expression and negligibly capable of individual expression. The human body functions according to the laws of nature, thus exhibiting average expression, but the human has exceptional capacities for individual expression and feelings which make greater purposeful activity possible.[69]

This system in Whitehead's philosophy is the basis for Charles Birch and John Cobb's discussion of gradations of value in nature. Birch and Cobb propose a theory of value that balances respect for each entity's intrinsic value with its instrumental value for others. Intrinsic value is richness of experience, the entity's enjoyment of its own experience.[70] Capacity for rich experience is determinative of any particular entity's value in the spectrum of value in nature. Although all entities have intrinsic value, their capacities for rich experience vary widely in proportion to their complexity, conscious feeling, and ability to entertain intensity of experience within individual unity. Because God derives divine rich experience from a universe of actual entities, presumably God experiences the value of entities differentially in terms of the rich experience that they add to God's experience. From a human perspective, the assessment of instrumental value in this theory does not differ significantly from modern hierarchical views that evaluate entities as means. The contribution of Birch and Cobb's theory of value is the presupposition of continuity among all grades of existents and concentration on the intrinsic value of all entities.

Applying these additional Whiteheadian concepts, Birch and Cobb construct gradations of value from Whitehead's four grades of existents. The inorganic aggregate grade has little intrinsic value and may be valued primarily in light of its instrumental value. The subjective experience of atoms and molecules has negligible intrinsic value; therefore, the intrinsic value of aggregates, such as rocks, is merely the sum of these slight values. The vegetable grade is a sophisticated organization of living cells, but the intrinsic value of plants is the value of the composite cells, since the plants do not have the unity of cells or the dominant occasion found in higher grades. The vegetable grade has higher intrinsic value than inorganic aggregates, but we may justifiably treat plants in terms of the significant instrumental value that they have for humans and other animals. Living cells which constitute vegetation cross a threshold into life. The intrinsic value of the vegetable living cell is more than the aggregation of the intrinsic values of its molecular constituents. The animal grade and humans have high intrinsic value and, on this basis, should not be valued primarily with respect to instrumental value. The complexity of subjective experience reaches new thresholds in animals and humans because of their highly evolved central nervous systems which enable conscious feeling. Consciousness heightens the capacity for rich experience. The intrinsic value of animals and humans is directly proportional to their individual capacities for or levels of rich experience.[71] The application of these gradations of value is to the general ethical principle that we should act to maximize rich experience by maximizing the quality of human life with minimum impact on nonhuman life.[72] This is part of a commitment to maximize value in general, including the value of the biosphere.

It is important to consider whether Birch and Cobb's theory refers to gradations of value or to a hierarchy in nature. The grades of existents to which Whitehead, Cobb, and Birch refer are not as discrete and distinct as the separations entailed in classical hierarchical thinking. In fact, there is not only a blurring of boundaries, but a clear overlap in both Whitehead's and Birch and Cobb's categories.

There are, however, features which suggest that the "gradations of value" actually constitute a hierarchy. The grades do indicate a ranking order on a spectrum from lower value to higher value. This ranking implies that some grades are inferior, whereas others are superior. The attachment of relative values to each grade is unambiguous in this regard. These gradations of value may be interpreted to indicate the superiority of human consciousness over the other centers of experience that compose the human body. In addition, humanity actually provides the criteria by which the various grades are judged. Humanity provides a standard or measure by which we are asked to evaluate other existents—Cobb and Birch establish the ranking of intrinsic value by the degree to which nonhumans in nature resemble human complexity in their nervous systems.[73] This in no way claims that only humans have value (or power associated with relative superiority), but like other hierarchical perspectives, it creates a chain of being from God to humanity to nonhuman animals, plants, and inorganic nature. In spite of its advances in recognizing value, subjectivity, and power in the nonhuman, does it really alter the basis on which we make particular decisions when choices between human and nonhuman interests are at stake?

I contend that the ethic that Birch and Cobb propose may be advanced within an ecofeminist antihierarchical stance. Birch and Cobb's ethic, which has much in common with ecofeminism, may not require its reference to gradations of value. I propose that we reexamine two features of Whitehead's thought that are relevant to a discussion of value: intensity and the lure of God. Value theory centered in these two ideas may give a different emphasis to an understanding of value in nature.

INTENSITY

The rich experience on which Birch and Cobb determine gradations of value is founded on the intensity of experience possible for any experiencing subject. According to Whitehead, every occasion aims at intensity of feeling in itself and in the relevant future.[74] Intensity may be understood as "the volume of life you can take into your being and still maintain your integrity and individuality."[75] More technically, it concerns how the multiplicity is felt by the one who is a subject-superject (the self-creating self that forms itself as an influence on future self-creating selves). When the multiplicity of occasions in its variety, breadth, and depth is entertained as contrasts, rather than incompatibilities, there is intensity of feeling.[76] The extreme example is God, who in the divine consequent nature entertains with immediacy the entire multiplicity without loss or discord. God experiences uninhibited intensity.[77] This interpretation of intensity with respect to the individual subject explains Birch and Cobb's perspective that entities who experience higher levels of intensity without discord or negative prehension of incompatibilities have more intrinsic value and contribute greater value to God (and the world).

From Whitehead's texts, however, it is possible to imagine an interpretation of intensity that focuses on the community rather than the individual subject.[78] Even at the subjective individual level, Whitehead notes the importance of intensity for the community—the aim of intensity is, in part, toward the relevant future. Whitehead's perspective is that the aim at intensity for the individual and the relevant future are not distinctly separated. The individual subject feels within itself the elements that will create intensity in the future and constitutes itself as a superject in anticipation of future intensity.[79] Beginning with this assumption that intensity is a term relevant to both the individual and the community, I propose that it is important to a feminist cosmology to explore the communal aspect of intensity while keeping the individual and communal aspects in balance.

If God's experience is analogous to the experience of other entities (and in process thought, it is), then I want to consider first what contributes intensity or rich experience to God's consequent nature. In Whitehead's understanding of God, God's primordial nature aims at the evocation of intensity in experiencing subject-superjects as a step toward God's own rich experience in the divine consequent nature.[80] God feels all experience as God's own. The multiplicity of experiences coalesce in God's consequent nature. Is it the case that God's rich experience depends primarily on the intensity of experience in an individual entity, or is it the case that the diversity in the world is the primary contributor to God's rich experience? I want to argue that it is the latter. The rich experience possible for God and for any future individuals would be diminished by the loss of entities less capable of entertaining contrasts in their unity. I hold that the diversity is equally as important as the intensity of any individual.

God derives rich experience from the intensity made possible by the multiplicity in the whole world. This shifts our emphasis to diversity in the world as a central source of intensity. Intensity, then, is more than just a determining factor in individual intrinsic value. An individual in its intrinsic value and instrumental value ought to be understood with respect to its contribution to the diversity of the whole.[81] After all, the intensity of experience in a human individual would be seriously diminished at the loss of birdsong or apples. In addition, few people would want to suggest that it would be valuable to overpopulate the world with humans capable of high intensity of experience in order to enhance overall intensity in the world and, consequently, in God. My ethical decisions about human and nonhuman issues must be guided by commitment to diversity and not only by respect for the level of intrinsic value in individuals.

LURE OF GOD

A discussion of intensity naturally brings us to a consideration of God's aim for rich experience in concrescing subjects. The initial aim (or initial phase of the subjective aim of the concrescing subject) originates with the primordial nature of God and fulfills God's purposes by acting as a lure toward intensity.[82] Given the actual world of the emerging entity, the initial aim is toward the best possible experience in the immediate moment. The initial aim is the lure of God toward the actualization of optimal potentiality. God's primordial nature, in response to the world, grades pure potentiality (the eternal objects) with respect to its relevance to the actual situation and introduces the resulting real possibility to the emerging occasion as a persuasive lure. In this regard, God is both the originator of novelty and the preserver of order.

Birch and Cobb, in their chapter "Life as God," refer to the activity of God in providing a lure for feeling. In defense of calling Life "God," they argue that Life is purposive, not only preserving order but advancing the cosmic aim for value. The purposive aim of Life is rich experience, life, and value in all things. We can say, then, that Life itself is purposeful. More than this, we may say that the purposes in all entities are derived from Life. The purposiveness of Life moves creatures beyond the givenness of the world toward a persuasive vision of unrealized possibility. The purposiveness of Life is part of the love of Life. The aims derived from Life are not abstract or generic; they are tailored to each entity in its specificity so that each entity may actualize the richest experience possible for its particular moment and circumstances. It is characteristic of this love that it does not favor any individual entity above another, but this love is for the actualizations of the best possibilities in every creature.[83]

Whitehead's position is that love is not the divine motivation behind the divine envisagement of the best possibilities for individuals.

> He [God], in his primordial nature, is unmoved by love for this particular, or that particular; for in this foundational process of creativity, there are no preconstituted particulars. . . . His tenderness is directed towards each actual occasion, as it arises.[84]

God loves creatures in their actuality rather than in their potentiality.

I would argue that God in God's primordial nature does express love for particulars in their potentiality and for persons, societies of actual entities, and enduring objects in their potentiality. A metaphor for this love is motherly love for her children. A mother loves her children both in their actuality and in their potentiality. Although there may be moments of disappointment when a child "is not working up to her potential," a mother continues to love the child for what she is capable of doing and seeks to persuade the child to take the next opportunity to fulfill her potential. This is true of the mother's love for each child. It is not that she loves only the child who achieves highest academic honors or the child who is a star athlete or the child who is an accomplished musician. She loves all her children and wishes each of them success in developing their aptitudes and talents. She acts as an encouragement, a lure toward their best futures. This does not mean that she favors one child over another or fosters their competition. Her love is not "equal"—not identically the same and not appropriate for comparison—for each child; she is touched profoundly by the uniqueness of each child and her love reflects this experience.

Because mother love entails the perception that the child is a person of value, it is a model for assessing value without resorting to hierarchy or gradations.[85] It is not a leveling of value, because it does not resort to attributing equal value to each child. Instead it perceives each child as of incomparable value, in the sense that it is inappropriate to compare the values of the individual children. The value of each child is unique and unsuited to comparison with another child. Similarly, God need not compare individuals' values. In expressing love and encouragement through the divine lure and in receiving each occasion into the divine life, God affirms the unique value of all creatures.

FEMINIST COSMOLOGY AND NATURE

This chapter proposes two nonhierarchical ways of assessing value that may contribute to a feminist relational ethic from a Whiteheadian perspective.

One reflects on the consequent nature of God, whereas the other reflects on the primordial nature of God. The first is intensity with respect to both individuals and the diversity; the second is potentiality.

How might these guides be applied to making practical decisions about our relationship with nature? Consider a practical example: the decision to choose either a vegetarian diet or a diet that includes meat. What factors are important in arriving at my decision? Concern for the intensity of experience of individuals requires me to consider, of course, that *my* nutritional needs be satisfied, but more important whether the lives of animals in both life and in death reflect humane treatment, some degree of freedom, and rich experience. Acknowledging the potentiality of all creatures, I must set aside human arrogance and realize that whether I consume vegetables, fruits, fish, poultry, or red meat, it must be done with a sense of the unique potentiality sacrificed and the sacredness of life, avoiding excesses that would be disrespectful of life. These considerations listed thus far conform with other discussions of this same issue, but consideration of diversity may add to the discussion. My concern for diversity leads me not only to question the circumstances under which animals are raised for food but to question the nature of corporate farming and agribusiness and to confront multiple exploitation of humans and nature. The effects of agribusiness on the environment—the result of salinization from irrigation, fertilization, spraying chemical pesticides and herbicides—may diminish diversity of regional plants and animals and limit the capacity of the land to support diversity. The exploitation of humans may diminish human potentiality and diversity—through exploitation of migrant workers, exacerbation of class differences by choices about land use, food distribution inequities on the local and global level, and increased risk of disease in human populations brought on by diet, pollution, or carcinogenic agricultural chemicals. The decision to become vegetarian, then, has added responsibilities that are overlooked without evaluating its effects on diversity. Both the suffering of the land and the suffering of animals (inclusive of humans) become my concern.

A Whiteheadian feminist cosmology entails guides for ethical decisions. First, diversity is a value to be cultivated within nature in its variety and among humans in their variety. Second, the unique potentiality of all existents in nature (including humans) requires that these existents be valued in and for themselves apart from their usefulness to others. Third, because of the continuity within nature and the ecological relationships within nature, values in nature and humanity are connected; therefore, choices should consider the contributions of existents to the well-being of other existents and the biosphere. Further, this continuity means that nature and culture are mutually implicated in sustaining the value and potentials of human, organic, and inorganic existents.

The dialogue between Whiteheadian thought and ecofeminism leads me to believe that each may be enriched by the other. Whiteheadian thought and feminist theologies and philosophies of nature (including ecofeminism) have in common the most important insights that there is continuity in nature, that nature is an interconnected web of interdependent creatures, and that diversity should be promoted in nature. Ecofeminism challenges process philosophy on the key issue of hierarchy. I have proposed that this need not be an obstacle to their compatibility, because there are interpretations of process thought that minimize or eliminate focus on value hierarchy in nature. This proposal refuses to separate the two natures of God, the primordial nature and the consequent nature. In God's primordial nature, God values creatures for their incomparable, unique value, as evidenced by the divine lure that promotes the actualization of individual potential. God in the consequent nature values creatures collectively for the intensity they contribute to God's rich experience and for the intensity they enable others to contribute to God's rich experience. From this perspective, our ethical decisions involve the knowledge that assessment of value is perspectival and must be undertaken with humility in respect for the sacredness and value of all nature. This modified Whiteheadian perspective contributes to feminism a concept of internal relatedness and a theological point of view from which to discuss value in nature.

NOTES

1. Sally Miller Gearhart, *The Wanderground: Stories of the Hill Women* (Boston: Alyson Publications, 1979).
2. Ibid., 2.
3. Ibid., 11.
4. Ibid., 43–52.
5. Ibid., 13.
6. Ibid., 11.
7. Ibid., 97.
8. Ibid., 13.
9. Ibid., 79.
10. Alice Walker, *The Color Purple* (New York: Washington Square Press, 1982), 178.
11. Joanna Macy, "Awakening to the Ecological Self," in *Healing the Wounds: The Promise of Ecofeminism*, ed. Judith Plant (Philadelphia: New Society Publishers, 1989), 202. Macy quotes John Seed, director of the Rainforest Information Center in Australia.
12. Carolyn Merchant, *The Death of Nature: Women, Ecology, and the Scientific Revolution* (San Francisco: Harper & Row, 1980), 2.
13. Vandana Shiva, "Development, Ecology, and Women," in *Healing the Wounds: The Promise of Ecofeminism*, ed. Judith Plant (Philadelphia: New Society Publishers, 1989), 84.

14. Susan Griffin, *Woman and Nature: The Roaring Inside Her* (New York: Harper & Row; Harper Colophon Books, 1978), 1.
15. Delores S. Williams, *Sisters in the Wilderness: The Challenge of Womanist God-Talk* (Maryknoll, N.Y.: Orbis Books, 1993), 108–9.
16. Ibid., 113.
17. Ibid., 116–17.
18. Ibid., 159.
19. Ibid., 160.
20. Patricia Hill Collins, *Black Feminist Thought: Knowledge, Consciousness, and the Politics of Empowerment* (New York: Routledge, 1990), 68–70.
21. Lynn White, "The Historical Roots of Our Ecologic Crisis," *Science* 155 (10 March 1967): 1205.
22. Susan Griffin, "Split Culture," in *Healing the Wounds: The Promise of Ecofeminism*, ed. Judith Plant (Philadelphia: New Society Publishers, 1989), 8.
23. Ibid.
24. Ibid., 9.
25. Ibid., 10–11.
26. Ibid., 13.
27. Starhawk, *Dreaming the Dark: Magic, Sex & Politics* (Boston: Beacon Press, 1982), 5.
28. Collins, *Black Feminist Thought*, 70.
29. Karen J. Warren, "The Power and the Promise of Ecological Feminism," *Environmental Ethics* 12, no. 2 (Summer 1990): 128.
30. Sherry B. Ortner, "Is Female to Male as Nature Is to Culture?" in *Woman, Culture, and Society*, ed. M. Z. Rosaldo and L. Lampere (Stanford: Stanford University Press, 1974), 73.
31. Rosemary Radford Ruether, *Sexism and God-Talk: Toward a Feminist Theology* (Boston: Beacon Press, 1983), 73–74.
32. Ibid., 75.
33. Ibid., 79.
34. Ibid., 80.
35. Ibid.
36. Ibid., 82–83.
37. Margo Adair and Sharon Howell, "The Subjective Side of Power," in *Healing the Wounds: The Promise of Ecofeminism*, ed. Judith Plant (Philadelphia: New Society Publishers, 1989), 219.
38. Ibid., 220.
39. Rachel Carson, *Silent Spring* (Boston: Houghton Mifflin Company, 1962), 297.
40. Ynestra King, "The Ecology of Feminism and the Feminism of Ecology," in *Healing the Wounds: The Promise of Ecofeminism*, ed. Judith Plant (Philadelphia: New Society Publishers, 1989), 18.
41. Ibid., 19.
42. Ibid., 24.
43. Ibid., 19–20.
44. Ibid., 22–23.
45. Donna Haraway, *Primate Visions: Gender, Race, and Nature in the World of Modern Science* (New York: Routledge, 1989).
46. The Biology and Gender Study Group, "The Importance of Feminist Critique for Contemporary Cell Biology," in *Feminism and Science*, ed. Nancy Tuana (Bloomington: Indiana University Press, 1985), 180–81.

47. Susan Thistlethwaite, *Sex, Race, and God: Christian Feminism in Black and White* (New York: Crossroad, 1989), 60.

48. Alfred North Whitehead, *Modes of Thought* (New York: Macmillan Company, 1938), 31.

49. Ibid.

50. Ibid., 34.

51. Ibid., 215.

52. Alfred North Whitehead, *Process and Reality: Corrected Edition*, eds. David Ray Griffin and Donald W. Sherburne (New York: Free Press, 1978), 109, 179.

53. Charles Birch and John B. Cobb Jr., *The Liberation of Life: From the Cell to the Community* (Cambridge: Cambridge University Press, 1981), 91.

54. Ibid., 92.

55. Ibid., 93.

56. Ibid., 98.

57. Alfred North Whitehead, *Adventures of Ideas* (New York: Free Press, 1967), 188.

58. Ibid.

59. Ibid., 176.

60. Ibid.

61. Susan Armstrong-Buck, "Nonhuman Experience: A Whiteheadian Analysis," *Process Studies* 18, no. 1 (Spring 1989): 1.

62. Whitehead, *Modes of Thought*, 32.

63. Ibid., 33–34.

64. Ibid., 34.

65. Ibid., 38.

66. Ibid.

67. Ibid., 39.

68. Ibid.

69. Ibid.

70. Birch and Cobb, *Liberation of Life*, 152.

71. Ibid., 152–53.

72. Ibid., 174.

73. Note comments such as: "a cell has experience of its world in some dim way analogous to our own, although we doubt that its experience is conscious. In short, its intrinsic value is far greater than that of its constitutive elements or of a stone. If a choice were to be made between a completely inorganic universe and a universe in which there was cellular life, there is no question but that the latter should be chosen." Ibid., 152.

74. Whitehead, *Process and Reality*, 27.

75. I take this phrase from Bernard Loomer, "S-I-Z-E," *Criterion* 13 (Spring 1974): 6.

76. Whitehead, *Process and Reality*, 83.

77. Ibid., 88.

78. This interpretation was suggested to me by Hans-Joachim Sander, visiting scholar at the Center for Process Studies, 1987–88.

79. Whitehead, *Process and Reality*, 27.

80. Ibid., 105.

81. Birch and Cobb also argue that diversity is important in a discussion of the rights of ecosystems.

All things have a *right* to be treated the way they *ought* to be treated for their own sake. But it is not possible to decide how to deal with an individual animal, species or ecosystem apart from a general view of the sort of world envisaged as being worth bringing into being. At this point a sense of the web of life, the value of diversity, and the way people are constituted by internal relations to others, will all guide the imagination.

Birch and Cobb, *Liberation of Life*, 170.
82. Whitehead, *Process and Reality*, 67.
83. Birch and Cobb, *The Liberation of Life*, 197–98.
84. Whitehead, *Process and Reality*, 105.
85. Jay B. McDaniel makes similar points in *Earth, Sky, Gods & Mortals: Developing an Ecological Spirituality* (Mystic, Conn.: Twenty-Third Publications, 1990), 68–69.

RELATING TO EACH OTHER

ARGUABLY, FEMINISM IS A movement engaged in critique of relationships, selective investment in relationships, and constructive thinking about relationships. Certainly, feminist scholarship offers critiques of social, political, economic, and personal relationships defined exclusively in patriarchal terms. The critiques of patriarchal relations are the high drama of feminism simplified in media caricatures as the war between the sexes. The limited public face of feminism hides two equally significant, and perhaps more significant, concerns of women scholars. First, feminist scholars are interested in questions of separatism and decisions about how to extricate themselves from patriarchal definitions of female gender. Feminists are concerned to select relationships that create hospitable contexts for self-definition and naming. Second, feminists are interested in constructing fresh definitions of female friendship and solidarity that resist patriarchal valuations of women's relationships. A hopeful, imaginative project, the vision of female friendship is challenged by the resistance of womanist scholars to the easy harmony of white feminist models that, in effect, makes women of color invisible.

In this chapter, my focus will minimize concern with the deconstruction of patriarchal relationships and emphasize the feminist selection of separatism and construction of female friendship. I am concerned to survey definitions of separatism and what separatism means for women's relationships. Separatism cannot be divided from the task of defining female friendship as valuable, noncompetitive, woman-centered relationships—and the task of understanding solidarity among white feminists and their womanist critics. Finally, my project is to suggest how separatism and female friendship are central to feminist cosmology.[1]

SEPARATISM AND ITS AMBIGUITY

In light of diversity among feminists, separatism is understood in a variety of ways and occasionally carries the vagueness of an intuition rather than the precision of a definition. At one level, separatism is represented by literary utopian visions (such as those of Sally Gearhart and Charlotte Perkins

Gilman) in which women form woman-identified, male-excluding communities. Feminist utopian literature depicts these hidden communities in isolation from patriarchal civilization which poses a threat to the creative and peaceful ecological niches imagined by women. These novels are, in fact, "useful fictions" that criticize patriarchy by envisioning alternatives to its misogynist, biocidal hierarchies. At their extremes, these alternatives capitalize on romanticization of a female essence and idealization of female community. Whether fictitious or theoretical, this type of separatism suggests that women's potential will be realized only when women have segregated themselves into gynophilic, biophilic women's societies.

Even within this much specificity, we could speculate about a number of forms that separatism might take. Separatist communities could be non-hierarchical or matriarchal, perhaps fluidly hierarchical or temporarily hierarchical. Women's separatist communities could be potentially inclusive of all women or selective of gyn/affectionate women and lesbians (perhaps of limited numbers of gynophilic men). These segregated women's communities could range from the profoundly nature-centered, nature-identified society of Sally Gearhart's utopia to the tidy, biophilic civilization imagined by Charlotte Perkins Gilman.

Perhaps a characterization of the hypothetical forms of feminist separatism would reflect the teleology of each. First, women might envision permanently segregated communities. In these societies, women could choose to separate themselves permanently from patriarchy in the effort to create an environment where women could experiment with personal and societal identity without the pervasive influence of patriarchy. This form of separatism would reflect despair about transcending patriarchy in society at large. Second, women could choose provisional separatism, segregating themselves for a time into exclusive women's communities as a means of deprogramming themselves from patriarchy. Provisional segregation could involve living in all-encompassing women's communities that reflect woman-identified priorities in business, domestic, and governmental affairs. This form of segregation would be temporary or provisional, either to allow women to form a metapatriarchal identity and then to reenter patriarchal society with renewed personal integrity or to await the transformation of patriarchy into postpatriarchy (provisional is a better descriptor for the latter purpose, because no feminist expects the imminent collapse of patriarchy). Third, instead of a total temporal and spatial segregation of women from patriarchy, women could and do engage in separatism that is limited to selected spheres of their lives. For example, women establish women's businesses, participate in consciousness-raising groups, reside in homes for battered women, create lesbian families, support women's political organizations. The purpose of nonsegregationist separatism is the formation of personal and political identity within patriarchal society.

These teleological characterizations make perfect sense; however, there is one serious flaw in the presupposition that leads to such categorizations within feminist separatism. This sort of categorization presupposes that the purpose of feminist separatism is fundamentally to answer the question, How do feminists intend to relate to men? It suggests that the issue basic to separatism is the female-male relationship. This is an androcentric interpretation of women's separatism. Perhaps, women's separatism is not a question of how women will relate to men but of how women intend to relate to each other.

DALY'S SEPARATISM AND BE-FRIENDING

Because Mary Daly is a wise prude who perseveres in removing androcentric, patriarchal scales from her own and other women's eyes, I want to refer to her understanding of radical feminist separatism as a gynocentric interpretation of women's separatism. Daly defines radical feminist separatism as "theory and actions of Radical Feminists who choose separation from the Dissociated State of patriarchy in order to release the flow of elemental energy and Gynophilic communication; radical withdrawal of energy from warring patriarchy and transferral of this energy to women's Selves."[2] Daly's definition suggests that separatism is not another investment of energy in confrontation with patriarchy. Separatism is the investment of energy in women's selfhood. It is precisely an absence of androcentric focus, a refusal to allow patriarchy to control the use of gynergy. Woman, not man, is the interest of separatism. "What about men?" is an irrelevant question, because separatism concentrates on a gynocentric agenda.

The solidarity of women who challenge patriarchy may create the superficial impression that feminists have already overcome the distortions in female relationships resulting from patriarchal oppression. In fact, this is not the case. Feminists have found it necessary to devote a good deal of effort to envisioning sisterhood and Gyn/affection. Recent literature indicates that the issue of female relationships is an unfinished constructive effort that will continue to receive priority.

If women are the more relational gender, why is it necessary for women to reflect on constructive modes of female relating? The fundamental reason is that the role of women as relational caretakers has been exercised for the nurturing of male/female relations rather than gynophilic relations. In this role, women have been instrumental in the maintenance of patriarchal relationships that serve to separate women from women. The result is that women are cast in competitive or estranged relationships with each other. Internalization of a patriarchal agenda leads women to do horizontal violence to each other. Mothers act as token torturers of their daughters when they teach their daughters to serve patriarchal interests. Token women, who have achieved apparent equality with men, take upon themselves the priorities of patriarchy (including nonrelational, gynophobic attitudes). Mary Daly has argued that patriarchy thrives on these separations of women. The patriarchal taboo against Women-Touching women is an indication that the power of female bonding is a threat to patriarchal strongholds.

Woman's estrangement is not simply from her sisters but also from herself. When Daly introduces the issue of separation or separatism in *Gyn/ Ecology*, it becomes clear that this estrangement is the crux of the issue. Using a play upon the etymology of "separate," Daly describes separatism as follows:

> When Spinsters speak of separatism, the deep questions that are being asked concern the problem of paring away from the Self all that is alienating and confining. Crone-logically prior to all discussion of political separatism from or within groups is the basic task of paring away the layers of false selves from the Self. In analyzing this basic Gyn/Ecological problem, we should struggle to detect whatever obstacles we can find, both internal and external, to this dis-covering of the Self.[3]

From this description of separatism, there are important features that ought to be underscored. First, separatism has nothing to do with building walls that isolate and confine women. It is primarily a concept that has to do with loosening the confinement of women. It is the release of women's energy and power. Second, separatism paradoxically removes that which is alienating. One could surmise from Daly's description that separatism facilitates genuine relationships with oneself and others rather than obstructing relationships. Third, separatism as the paring away of false selves from the Self is prior to any discussion of separatism from or within groups. Political separatism is a derivative issue, not the primary issue. Fourth, separatism intends to remove both internal and external barriers to selfhood. Removal of internal obstacles is crone-logically primary for all authentic separation and is normative for personal and political separatism.

In her book *Pure Lust*, an elemental feminist philosophy, Daly discusses separatism in relationship to Be-Friending, a term that suggests the ontological status of female friendship. Radical feminist separatism is defined here as "a necessary disposition toward separation from the causes of fragmentation; especially: advocacy of withdrawal from all parasitic groups (as a church), for the purpose of gynophilic/biophilic communication."[4]

In this definition, once again the point is that women have already been fragmented and that separatism is action that counters phallic separatism, separation of women from ourselves and our Selves. Fragmentation is the result of broken gynophilic, biophilic communication—the ontological communication of deep and natural interconnectedness. Fragmentation is the disconnectedness that flies in the face of interconnectedness, interruption of the flow of connection with all be-ing. The philosophical and existential presupposition is that "everything that IS is connected with everything else that IS."[5] Fragmentation creates "things" that are disconnected from Ultimate Reality and participation in be-ing. In this sense, they are nonbe-ing. In another sense, these things are very real barriers to realization of be-ing, barriers from which women must separate themselves.

Daly suggests that the word "separatism" functions as a Labrys. It has a two-edged meaning. "Separatism" names phallic separatism, the separatism that blocks women's lust for ontological communication. "Separatism" also names feminist resistance to phallic separatism. Positively stated, it is woman's choice for radical connectedness in biophilic be-ing. Radical feminist separatism is transcendence of the fear of separation from phallic separators and acknowledgment that separation from Self has already happened. Radical feminist separatism is a choice to pare away the false selves layered upon women's selfhood by patriarchy and to undertake telic centering, the purposive focusing that facilitates women's metamorphosis.

To focus on radical feminist separatism is to concern ourselves with a second order term. Separatism is not the primary women's movement. The ontological metamorphosis of women is the final cause of women—it is women's movement. Because the movement of women is blocked by patriarchy, separatism is an essential prerequisite to metamorphosis. Metamorphosis, biophilic communication, participation in Be-ing are women's movement. Metamorphosis contextualizes separatism.

In Daly's sense, separation is unrelated to boundaries and walls, because sisterhood is concerned with eliminating walls and expanding physical and psychic space. Separation or separatism is the paring away of alienating, confining false selves in order that women may break through both internal and external obstacles to dis-covering the Self. Women have experienced similar forms of oppression under patriarchy, but the paring process occurs in a variety of expressions that reflect unique histories and temperaments among women. There is no equality/identity among unique Selves. Acknowledging the differences in Selves is a painful necessity for sisters. Such differences mean that women may need separation from other Female Selves in order to make their unique discoveries.

Pain is part of experiencing the differences among women and of choosing separation, but there is also potential in differences and separation.

Acknowledging the deep differences among friends/sisters is one of the most difficult stages of the Journey and it is essential for those who are Sparking in free and independent friendship rather than merely melting into mass mergers. Recognizing the chasms of differences among sister Voyagers is coming to understand the terrifying terrain through which we must travel together and apart. At the same time, the spaces between us are encouraging signs of our immeasurable unique potentialities, which need free room of their own to grow in, to Spark in, to Blaze in. The greatness of our differences signals the immensity/intensity of the Fire that will flame from our combined creative Fury.[6]

Woman-identified relationships entail the authentic likeness against which genuine differences may emerge. Woman-identified relationships, therefore, create new and varying patterns of relating, subject to the intensity and turbulence of unique Female Selves in relationship.[7]

The purpose of radical feminist separatism is provision of a context that promotes gynophilic communication. It affirms the identity of women as original women, women who are the antithesis of man-made female creations, women who are self-originating. Separatism is a communal process that facilitates the flow of interconnectedness for each woman.

Be-Friending is an ontological category for Daly that describes the context or atmosphere within which women experience metamorphosis. Be-Friending is ontological friending; radical ontological, biophilic communication among women, implying the interconnectedness of all be-ing.[8]

Be-Friending promotes the creation of an atmosphere for leaps of metamorphosis. The Websters who weave the contexts for metamorphosis are inspired by female potential, female potency/power. Any woman who makes leaps of metapatterning weaves a network of Be-Friending.[9]

Be-Friending is creative for women in two ways that parallel two dimensions of separatism. First, Be-Friending is creative for individual women for whom separatism is the dis-covery of genuine selfhood, which has been submerged beneath layers of pseudoselfhood. In this case, Be-Friending means that each woman becomes a friend to her own be-ing. Be-Friending encourages woman to actualize her capacities to the fullest, including her capacity for participation and activity in a metamorphic context with other women. When a woman befriends (Be-Friends) herself/her Self, her energy is redirected. She no longer expends energy in the maintenance of patriarchy and in her own dissociated, disintegrated selfhood. An individual woman in the process of finding her personal integrity and focused selfhood also experiences the focusing of her energy, which, Daly claims, releases her rage. Rage is a positive attribute, an ontological Passion; Be-Friending sustains outrage as a transformative, focusing force and a source for creative activism on behalf of herself and other women.[10] Thus, Be-Friending is creative of and for the individual woman who becomes creative for other women. It follows that, in a second way, Be-Friending is creative for the sisterhood of women for whom separatism is for the purpose of gynophilic/biophilic communication. Be-Friending requires a context for the emerging, metamorphosing identities of women. It is an atmosphere of encouragement (en-couragement) that creates female friendship. The two creative dimensions of Be-Friending require each other. Daly describes Be-Friending as a "Spiraling" movement. As a woman's genuine selfhood emerges, it beckons the emergence of genuine selfhood in another. Woman becomes a friend to herself and to her sisters, and so Be-Friending is something of a contagion of epidemic proportions.

Be-Friending reveals the uniqueness of female friendship in comparison with male comradeship. While the comradeship/fraternity survives by draining women of their energy, female friendship is a bonding that is energizing/gynergizing.[11] Female bonding is threatening to comradeship, because it is a relationship that ignores the brotherhood and exposes its relationships with women as property arrangements. Female bonding is a free bondage. "The radical friendship of Hags means loving our own freedom, loving/ encouraging the freedom of the other, the friend, and therefore *loving freely*."[12]

Women are in the process of discovering what it means to be together as women. If women assume that sisterhood is similar to brotherhood with respect to freedom and self-affirmation, then the struggle to understand female bonding results in an imitation of male comradeship/brotherhood. On the contrary, sisterhood can only be described with words like "Sparking of Female Selves," "New Be-ing," and "biophilic Self-finding."[13] Sisterhood refers to the wide range of female relating that extends to women of similar vision, who may never have come into acquaintance. Friendship is a potential for all sisters/friends. Female-identified erotic love is one expression of radical female friendship.[14] Sisterhood, female friendship, and female-identified erotic love are female discoveries of relationships that do not entail the self-loss of male-defined relationships for women.

Lesbianism is not merely a "special case" of sisterhood or female friendship. For Daly, it is the paradigm. Lesbianism refers to woman-identified women who have rejected false loyalties to men.[15] Lesbian communities, because of their marginal status, are somewhat beyond reach of patriarchal influence and act as pioneers in the dis-covering of female friendship. Lesbianism is ultimately threatening to patriarchy because it is more than physical contact between women. The Total Taboo against Women-Touching women is rooted in patriarchal fear of the gynergized power among interconnected, touching women—"For Women-Touching women are the seat of a tremendous power which is transmissible to other women by contact."[16]

Be-Friending, as feminists have already seen, is not a panacea for women. The very diversity implied by female friendship means that there is potential for conflict and disappointment. Be-Friending does not mean that every woman is a friend to every other woman. In the first place, time and energy for friendship are limited. In the second place, temperament and circumstances prevent women from being friends. For Be-Friending to take place, women must be able, first, to identify women who are *for* women and, second, to identify from among these women those with whom Elemental friendship is possible. That all women, even those who are *for* women, cannot be intimate elemental friends is no cause for despair, because all women can participate and communicate in female friendship.

Although friendship is not possible among all feminists, the work of Be-Friending can be shared by all, and all can benefit from this Metamorphospheric activity. Be-Friending involves Weaving a context in which women can Realize our Self-transforming, metapatterning participation in Be-ing. Therefore it implies the creation of an atmosphere in which women are enabled to be friends. Every woman who contributes to the creation of this atmosphere functions as a catalyst for the evolution of other women and for the forming and unfolding of genuine friendships.[17]

The character of female friendship may be inferred from the basic premise that biophilic relationships occur among woman-identified women. For Daly, sisterhood is primarily the relationship of lesbian women and secondarily of gyn/affectionate women (who for various reasons in a complex world also maintain relationships with men). From this starting point emerge the particular characteristics of Be-Friending. First, relationships must facilitate the dis-covery of Self through Self-acceptance and Separation. Second, relationships are multidimensional, so that to speak of Women-Touching women implies an interconnectedness inclusive of physical contact but not exclusively physical. Third, relationships are creative and gynergizing by virtue of the power of Be-Friending.[18]

Clearly, Daly powerfully moves women to examine concretely the necrophilic patriarchal relationships that have diminished and victimized women. Then, metaphorically, Daly has constructed a transforming vision of female relating. Its value is precisely that women are creatively empowered and reunited with their Selves and other Female Selves from whom patriarchy has alienated them.

RAYMOND'S SEPARATISM AND GYN/AFFECTION

By reference to Janice Raymond, we may summarize and restate the same problematic with a different vocabulary that helps to illuminate issues at stake. Raymond proposes that the dominant worldview may be accurately named hetero-reality. This perspective supports the perception that "woman exists always in relation to man" and, consequently, the perception that women together are actually women alone.[19] Hetero-reality is created by the prevailing system of hetero-relations that expresses a range of social, political, and economic relations established between men and women *by men.* Paradoxically, women are used instrumentally to sustain hetero-relations when, in fact, reality is homo-relational; that is, male-male relations actually determine the course of reality in social, political, and economic spheres. The result is that women's energy is expended in support of hetero-relations. Under the assumptions of hetero-relations, the only relationships of consequence for women are male-female relationships. Hetero-reality assumes that women do not/ought not have relationships with each other of primary social and political importance, because, by hetero-relational gender definitions, women-women relationships are not valuable or powerful.

Raymond proposes that this is the basis of the need for a philosophy of female affection (the project of her book *A Passion for Friends*). Women, who have been monopolized by maintaining relationships with men, now must reflect on what it means for women to move beyond the hetero-relational separation of women toward gyn/affectionate relationships. Gyn/affectionate relationships are relations of woman-to-woman attraction, influence, and movement. "Gyn/affection" is a term that elucidates the meaning of female friendship. It refers to the passion that women feel toward each other. This passion is an attraction for women *as* women, that is, an attraction for women not as women defined by hetero-relations but as women who are shaping their genuine selfhood.

Female friendship has its origin with original women—women who chart their own "beginnings from the deepest recesses of [their Selves] and other women."[20] Female friendship is a context within which women may regain the integrity of their disintegrated Selves and restore the prime order of women in women's relationships. Gyn/affection is a context within which women may remember original women. To explain the meaning of "original woman," we must avoid confusing the term with either a romanticized, essentialist archetype or an imaginative, theoretical or exemplary prototype. Original woman is not derivative and is not to be imitated. Raymond uses the word "original" in the sense of creation. An original woman is not created by men who fashion hetero-reality but by herself. Female friendship helps to create original women, but it is original woman who is the beginning of female friendship. The woman who invents herself has created her primary friendship with herself, and this act is enabling of friendship with other women. Original woman is in relation with herself and other original women.

With respect to the word "separatism," Raymond considers the variety of ways that feminist theorists define the term. If we mean by "separation" the idea of segregation, then Raymond finds it necessary to make some significant distinctions.[21] Raymond clearly rejects sex-segregation, which is an option not obtained by women's choice, but against their will. This is an imposed ghettoization of women. Separation that occurs by women's choice needs to be distinguished from segregation. Separatism must also be distinguished from simplistic, escapist, apolitical dissociation from the world. Separatism is not to be understood as "escape from"—separatism is a move toward personal integrity. It is not a dissociation from the world, but a dissociation from hetero-reality. The purpose of separatism is movement toward woman-identified existence that is marked by worldliness and the intent to make a difference in the world.

As Raymond argues, we must be careful about what we mean by dissociation of women. Women have developed a passive dissociation from the world by virtue of the fact that the world and its politics are man-made, homo-relational. Women who have been caretakers of hetero-relations have not participated in world making. Women, therefore, have been worldless by default. In addition, there are women who have chosen worldlessness as a feminist ideal. The difficulty in both types of dissociation is that female existence becomes segregated, and women lose access to the world. By dissociation, women multiply their superfluousness in a world that already views women as superfluous.[22] Dissociation also diffuses the purpose and power of female friendship in two respects. First, it precludes the potential of female friendship to replace hetero-reality. Second, and perhaps more important, dissociation entails dissociation from women. Thus, Gyn/affection is restricted to a small community of women. Dissociation makes Gyn/affection a personal rather than a political matter.

Raymond emphasizes the active political character of female friendship. The dissociation, which Raymond criticizes as the segregation of women or as apolitical, worldless separatism, robs female friendship of its political power and makes it a personal matter only. Women who are separated from the world cannot cultivate female friendships that have the capacity to change the world. Female friendship is both personally and politically important for women, because it provides definition and concreteness for disenfranchised women. As such, female friendship is the basis of women's political power and vantage point.

> Friendship gives women a point of crystallization for living in the world. It gives form, shape, and a concrete location to women who have no state or geographical homeland and, in fact, no territorial ghetto or diaspora from which to act. Friendship provides women with a common world that becomes a reference point for location in a larger world. The sharing of common views, attractions, and energies gives women a connection to the world so that they do not lose their bearing. Thus a sharing of personal life is at the same time a grounding for social and political existence. By the same token, anything that militates against women's-being-in-the-world—against female worldliness—undermines a strong female friendship that has political consequences, namely, Gyn/affection.[23]

The political significance of female friendship is so essential that Raymond believes that friendship is sacrificed apart from a commitment to worldliness—"Worldlessness produces friendlessness."[24]

Gyn/affection creates both personal and political space for women. It is the space within which a woman lives *"as a woman, among women, among men."*[25] Women together, through female friendship, envision a world truly inclusive of feminism and the growth of women and, at the same time, create personal space for the actualization of women's potential. Female friendships are relationships among women who are insider outsiders. Insider outsiders function on the boundary of the man-made world and are grounded by female friendship as they live within the tension between the world created by men and the world imagined by women.[26] The insider outsider is neither assimilated into the world nor victimized by it; she maintains her personal integrity (through support from female friendship) without resorting to worldless dissociation.

> The insider outsider lives in the world with worldly integrity, weaving the strands of feminist wisdom into the texture of the world and paving the way for the entrance of women as women, that is, women on our own terms, into the world. As an inside outsider, a woman's work is characterized by the dual tension between her feminism and her worldliness. Her worldliness is dependent on her feminist vision, yet her feminist vision is actualized in her worldly location.[27]

Raymond advocates a feminist politics based on female friendship. Gyn/affection is not merely for the purpose of forming personal bonds of friendship. It has a social/political/economic function for the purpose of empowering women.

HUNT'S JUSTICE-SEEKING FRIENDS

If "the personal is political" resonated through 1970s feminism, "female friendship is political" resounds through 1980s and current feminist philosophy and theology—and Mary E. Hunt provides a model for female friendship as political in *Fierce Tenderness: A Feminist Theology of Friendship.*[28] Hunt resists any notion that female friendship is merely a privatized event without value or power. She presumes that the personal relationship of female friendship is a political activity, because the mutual responsibility that friends have for each other is a public activity and because friendship is one component of social relationships. The political character of female friendships is not simply an incidental quality of friendships. In part, female friendship is defined by its politics: Friendship is "those voluntary human relationships that are entered into by people who intend one another's well-being and who intend that their love relationship is part of a justice-seeking community."[29]

Women's friendships—among family members, neighbors, couples, groups, and communities—is revelatory. First, women's friendships reveal something about ourselves to us. Within the context of female friendships, friends discover that they are loving persons. The gifts of friendship are self-knowledge and self-awareness that lead to self-love. Second, women's friendships reveal something about each other to those who are friends. Friendship is a context for discovering what is lovable in another and knowing the other as loving. Third, women's friendships reveal something about the natural world. Friends discover in the natural order what it means to love differences. Female friendship is the paradigm from which we learn to befriend the earth and its inhabitants. Finally, female friendships reveal something about the divine by suggesting a new metaphor and relationship with God/ess, She who is Mother.[30]

Hunt argues that marriage and heterosexual coupling provide a problematic model for Christian values, and she proposes a model of female friendship that can move Christianity toward justice, because of the ethical paradigm that friendship entails. Love, power, embodiment, and spirituality are the four elements that comprise the model. The four elements are mutually interrelated and are implicated in each other such that each interfaces with all the others. When the four elements are balanced and reciprocally engaged, there is generativity in the friendship, and each friend receives something new. The model accounts for human frailty and imperfection in friendships, because the elements, out of balance, lead to stress, tension, and the termination of friendship.[31]

Each of the four elements contributes value to the friendship. First, love provides a sense of connection to the friend. It is *"an orientation toward the world as if my friend and I were more united than separated, more at one among the many than separate and alone."*[32] Love is the urge for unity without the loss of individuality. Second, power refers to the source of empowerment in friendship. Power is described as *"the ability to make choices for ourselves, for our dependent children, and with our community."*[33] It describes personal agency without resorting to unilateral, nonreciprocal, competitive, or disconnected definitions of power. Friendship, as a consequence, is transformative of social structures and even of power itself. Third, embodiment creates the context and attitudes necessary for health and pleasure. Embodiment is central to friendship, because *"virtually everything we do and who we are is mediated by our bodies."*[34] Healthy embodiment frees friends from limited focus on genital pleasure that is typical of the marriage metaphor. Fourth, spirituality moves friends from a privatized world of spirit toward the community. Very broadly, spirituality is *"making choices about the quality of life for oneself and for one's community."*[35] These are neither trivial nor personal choices but profound choices for the sake of friendship, justice, and ethics.

Hunt's model has breadth. The model is flexible enough to allow for a wide range of friendships available to everyone. The model is not fixed but accommodates the ambiguous nature of friendships that are complex, changing, and "messy." It is not limited to advocacy of limited types of friendship identified by quantitative elements (such as heterosexuality). Instead the model recognizes friendship in the qualitative experiences of relationship, and in the elements of attention, generativity, and community characteristic of female friendship.[36]

The energy and promise of this model are best indicated by the justice-seeking that issues from female friendship. Hunt describes female friendship as justice-seeking contexts on a number of grounds. Historically, women friends have brought about social change (for example, Susan B. Anthony and Elizabeth Cady Stanton among many others). Women friends are life-lines that enable survival (in childrearing, in crisis, in poverty, in hopelessness). Because women form coalitions that seek justice, Hunt argues that female friendship provides a new ethical norm.[37]

As a new ethical norm, Hunt's model faces its true test: Can this model deliver a justice-seeking ethic? Hunt experiments with the model as a critique of established Christian ethical paradigms. First, Hunt suggests that the model is applicable to a critique of female-male relationships. By comparison, the shared, reciprocal attention of female friendships is critical of the inequality of female-male relations. In its creativity, female friendship underscores the limitations of female-male generativity defined by reproduction. Female friendship unmasks a hunger for community lurking in the privatization of female-male relations.[38] Second, Hunt applies the model to ecological relationships. Avoiding the ethical shortcomings of a parent-child metaphor, female friendship suggests that an ecological ethic requires respect and equality toward nature.[39] Third, as a norm for social ethics, female friendship offers foreign policy critique, and as a global model, it transforms structures and power relationships. Nations as "friends" form justice-seeking coalitions that work toward bodily health and safety, balanced power dynamics, quality of life, and respect, even love, for the uniqueness of others.[40]

A self-critical scholar, Hunt is aware of the potential shortcomings of this model. She notes that mystery, grace, and surprise, which create and sustain relationships, are not accounted for in the model. She also notes that analyzing relationships using the model is not equivalent to spiraling into future relationships and new experiences. Perhaps most important, given Hunt's sensitivity to profound differences among women, she notes the limitations of the model imposed by its starting point in women's experience. Her critique is that the model may be bound to gender, class, race, and culture specificity. The model may not transfer well to female-male or male-male friendships. In addition, the model may not transfer well to all female friendships and may obstruct other women's evaluation of and creativity in friendship.[41]

WOMANISTS, SISTERS, AND COMMUNITY

White feminist theory, especially informed by lesbian experience, tells us a lot about female friendship, but not about all female friendship. Womanist literature and African-American scholarship write different dimensions of female friendship and community.

Womanist literature is abundant in female friendships that empower women, resist domination, acknowledge conflict, and enable survival. In Zora Neale Hurston's *Their Eyes Were Watching God*, Janie's grandmother Nanny wishes her own dreams into Janie's future and teaches Janie what she needs to know to survive and resist—"De nigger woman is de mule uh de world so fur as Ah can see. Ah been prayin' fuh it tuh be different wid you."[42] Janie's friend Phoeby hears Janie into self-revelation and speaks on Janie's behalf—"Dat's just de same as me 'cause mah tongue is in mah friend's mouf."[43] Janie's lover and friend, Tea Cake, "was a glance from God" who called her soul "out from its hiding place."[44] Alice Walker's *The Color Purple* writes itself from friendships between sisters (Celie and Nettie), between lovers (Celie and Shug), and among women (Celie, Shug, Sofia, Mary Agnes). Ntozake Shange's novel *Sassafrass, Cypress, and Indigo* weaves the story of Hilda Effania's befriending of her daughters through her affection and support for them, through the creativity that she shares with them, and through lessons in surviving as an African-American woman.[45] If anything, womanist literature teaches us that friendships warmed by African-American women are complex, unvarnished, and pluriform.

Feminist/womanist theorists make women's relationships significant in the shape of gender, race, and class interpretation and analysis that forms their work. African-American women's relationships are a thematic thread running through *Black Feminist Thought* by Patricia Hill Collins. One premise of Collins's book complements other feminist observations: Women come to voice in the safe space created by women's relationships.[46] Collins notes that black women connect with each other in both formal and informal ways. Formally, black women have enabled politically significant communities in the black church and black women's organizations, such as sororities and women's clubs. Informally, black women's relationships, no less empowering and important, have coalesced among friends and within families between mothers, daughters, and sisters. Collins describes mother-daughter relationships as those relationships that give daughters survival knowledge and the relationships of sisters and friends as connections that mutually affirm the full humanity, value, and entitlement of women.[47]

Collins identifies two particular types of relationships among black women, which I recognize as distinctive of black women's relationships when compared with white women's relationships. First, othermothers are women in extended parenting relationships with bloodmothers' children. Othermothers may be grandmothers, sisters, aunts, cousins, or neighbors who assist bloodmothers with child care, thus forming a network of support for both children and other women. Othermothers who are teachers develop "mothering the mind" relationships with black women students that nurture an Afrocentric worldview, self-reliance, and vision toward alternative futures for young black women.[48] Not only does the othermother relationship suggest a communal model of neighborhood parenting, but, as sociologist Cheryl Gilkes notes, the othermother network may be the stimulus for black women to be activists in defense of black children's health and well-being.[49] Collins writes that

> Black women's experiences as othermothers provide a foundation for Black women's political activism. Nurturing children in Black extended family networks stimulates a more generalized ethic of caring and personal accountability among African-American women who often feel accountable to all the Black community's children.[50]

The relationships of othermothers, bloodmothers, and children embodies a feminist Afrocentric, caring, community-centered ethic conducive to political activism and antithetical to models of childrearing based on privatization and property relations.

A second relationship distinct among African-American women is the connection among African-American women who do not know each other; that is, there is solidarity and recognition among African-American women who are strangers to each other but who value each other and who share similar experiences and, perhaps, common struggles.[51] Coincidental encounters are the contexts for affirmation of value and encouragement to realize potentials. Crossing lines of class, neighborhood, and familiarity, African-American women experience pride and self-affirmation in the ability to support and rejoice in the accomplishments of others.

Womanists describe these relationships as characteristic of sisterhood, but these types do not exhaust the rich variety of relationships that enter African-American women's experience, and we should not assume that all womanists choose to engage in identical types of relationships. Certainly how womanists choose to relate to white feminists is an example of how diverse African-American women's choices about sisterhood may be. One interpretation of sisterhood and the relationship of African-American women to white U.S. feminists is indicated by Patricia Hill Collins's understanding of the term "womanist." Collins describes womanist movement as humanist movement. When Collins teases out Alice Walker's definition of "womanist," she notes in particular the universalist character of black feminism:

> traditionally universalist, as in "Mama, why are we brown, pink, and yellow, and our cousins are white, beige, and black?" Ans.: "Well, you know the colored race is just like a flower garden, with every color flower represented."[52]

Collins reads Walker's definition as testimony to the universalism of black feminism: "Walker universalizes what are typically seen as individual struggles while simultaneously allowing space for autonomous movements of self-determination."[53]

By other accounts, however, black feminist movement realizes the ambivalence among black women toward sisterhood with white women. Bell hooks observes the reasons that African-American women resist feminist sisterhood with Euro-American women. Some reasons are rooted in a lingering sexism in bourgeois white feminism. Hooks observes that white feminist preoccupation with victimization retains the male supremacist view that to be female is to be a victim. The identification of femaleness with victimization is inhospitable to assertive, strong women—and therefore, hooks argues, to black women whose sisterhood is based on shared strengths and resources.[54] More generally, African-American women express a justifiable distrust of white feminist movement because of unexamined racism. Angela Davis, for example, constructs an argument in *Women, Race and Class* based on the living memory of white women's betrayal and racism as slave mistresses, abolitionists, and suffragists.[55] The constructive honesty of womanist theological critique holds contemporary white feminist theology accountable for its racism. Jacquelyn Grant, in *White Women's Christ and Black Women's Jesus*, after a responsible analysis of white feminist theology, notes two problems that mark feminist theology as white if not also racist: limitation to white women's experience as a resource and control of the definition of feminism and feminist movement without acknowledging that white women's experience is universalized and renders nonwhite women's experience invisible.[56] Theologians Delores Williams and Kelly Brown Douglas identify commonalities with white feminist thought, yet similarly criticize a tendency toward one-dimensional gender analysis that neglects white women's racism and classism.[57] Although suspicion and criticism of white feminism are reasonable, womanists and black feminists do not necessarily resort to separatism from white feminists. After a scathing, impassioned criticism of white feminism, for example, bell hooks invites white women to solidarity and transformation on the condition that white women acknowledge the racism of feminist movement by making radical gestures to eliminate racism, by learning black women's culture, by respecting differences, by redistributing wealth, and by moving toward collective rather than individual concerns.[58] Embracing differences is the key to solidarity. "Women do not need to eradicate difference to feel solidarity. We do not need to share common oppression to fight equally to end oppression."[59] Far from cultivating fear, anger, or guilt, confrontation is the beginning of revolutionary change.[60]

Although it would be a mistake to think that theologies by nonwhite women are identical, it is unmistakable that similar criticisms of white feminism, along with aspirations for a transformed solidarity among women, are voiced by *mujerista*, Asian feminist, and Jewish feminist theologians. Jewish feminist Judith Plaskow has expressed the tension between inclusion with and appropriation of dominant white Christian feminist discourse and cooptation of a sometimes decontextualized Jewish tradition. Plaskow reinforces the point that white Christian feminism has controlled feminist theological discourse at the same time that she acknowledges that she has benefited from the power of inclusion in white feminist discourse.[61] Chinese Christian feminist Kwok Pui-lan restates the criticism that white feminism makes nonwhite women's experience invisible when she writes, "I too, have great difficulty when I hear white feminists use Asian resources in an uncritical way.... The suffering and pain of Asian sisters become invisible if we romanticize Asian religious traditions."[62] Cuban-American *mujerista* theologian Ada María Isasi-Díaz uses the phrase "invisible invisibility" to describe totally ignoring the being of Hispanic women.

> Those who totally ignore us do not even know they are doing so; they are incapable of acknowledging our presence. "Invisible invisibility" questions the very existence of Hispanic women; it makes us question not only the value of our specificity but the very reality of it.[63]

Isasi-Díaz adds an important observation that even white feminist "respect" for *mujerista* theology is a mask that avoids engaging difference and interacting meaningfully.[64] Isasi-Díaz and African-American womanist Toinette Eugene concur in their advocacy of a genuinely pluralistic feminism.[65] This important consensus about the need to decenter white women's experience from feminism is not to disvalue white women's experience but to dismantle white Christian feminist supremacy.

Third World feminists and womanists write differently than Euro-American feminists about women's relationships with women and also about women's relationships with men. For African-American womanists, Alice Walker's definition of womanist reflects and shapes talk about women's relationships with men. "Sometimes loves individual men, sexually and/or nonsexually. Committed to survival and wholeness of entire people, male *and* female.

Not a separatist, except periodically, for health."[66] For womanist theologian Kelly Brown Douglas, the phrase "commitment to survival and wholeness of entire community" is pivotal. Black women's experience is not fragmented but concerned with the welfare and freedom of women, men, and children. Douglas's multidimensional and bifocal analysis of black oppression provides one example of how African-American womanists address the issues of separatism and female-male relationships. Douglas's analysis is multidimensional, because it examines how race, class, gender, and sexual oppression intersect to affect black community. Her analysis is bifocal, because it names how the black community perpetuates black oppression through racism, classism, sexism, and heterosexism. External and internal sources of oppression alienate black community.[67] To ensure wholeness in the community, black women must not limit their concern to gender issues (as black male liberation theologians have tended to limit concern to race issues), but black women must, for example, confront rap music when, at its worst, it is abusive of women, even as black women affirm rap music when, at its best, it functions as critical cultural expression.[68] Interpreted in relation to womanist theology, black women's experience, as Delores Williams observes, enlarges all Christian theological discourse. Womanist theology "opposes all oppression based on race, sex, class, sexual preference, physical disability and caste."[69] Womanist theology criticizes equally black male oppression of black women and white racism that oppresses black women and men. White feminist critique of patriarchy is inadequate to analyze multilayered oppression and is silent about the role of class and race privilege in the relationships of white women and African-American women.[70] Although womanist theology occupies a unique niche as a multitasked theology, it is usually nonseparatist and dialogical, welcoming genuine dialogue among diverse theological voices.[71]

In her instructive survey of Asian women's theology, Chung Hyun Kyung, a Korean feminist theologian, writes that Asian women's integrity requires connection between liberation of women and liberation of men. "Asian women cannot set aside their liberation as women and struggle for democracy or against classism and racism as if the liberation process can be chopped up into different pieces."[72] Asian women stress that feminist revolution cannot happen for them apart from their children and men, because women and men have endured colonialism, neocolonialism, exploitation, militarism, and victimization together and must struggle and have struggled historically as a community for democracy, nationalism, and socialist changes. Reciprocally, Asian liberation movements must entail women's liberation under terms defined by Asian women rather than at the convenience of men's agendas for revolution.[73] Although the aim of Asian feminism is communal, Asian feminist analysis entails critique of men's betrayal of women.

For example, their fathers are supposed to be the protectors, the ones who give Asian women safety in an oppressive world, providing food, shelter, and clothing. But too often Asian women are beaten by their fathers or sold into child marriage or prostitution. Asian women's husbands are supposed to love them, but frequently they batter their wives in the name of love and family harmony. Asian women's brothers are supposed to support and encourage them, but they instead often further their own higher educations by tacitly using their Asian sisters, ignoring the reality that their sisters are selling their bodies to pay for tuition. The promises of safety, love, and nurturing have not been fulfilled. Asian women have trusted their beloved men, but their men have often betrayed them.[74]

Third World and U.S. womanist, feminist, and *mujerista* theologies add depth and complexity to analysis of women's relationships. Not least of the contributions are commitments to solidarity and self-critique. A first point is that solidarity among Third World women who are theologians is supported and enacted by organizations such as the Women's Commission of the Ecumenical Association of Third World Theologians. U.S. womanist theologian Kelly Brown Douglas includes solidarity with the global oppressed community of people of color as part of her multidimensional analysis of wholeness. Douglas advocates continuing dialogue between African-American womanists ("Third World women trapped in the First World") and Third World women living in Third World countries as women sort out their differences and the dilemma created by identifying African-American women with the First World.[75] A further point is that solidarity is tested by the educational status and privilege of women who are theologians and women in Christian congregations. The challenges for African-American womanist theologians is to be accountable to black women in the church and community, where empowerment, teaching, and dialogue are critical.[76] Chung writes compassionately about the separation of educated women theologians from poor women.

Many educated women theologians in Asia know that they are not doing theology *for* the poor women. They articulate theology in order to enhance the liberation process in their broken communities, seeking the common future of the communities. These women do theology as a form of repentance and self-criticism. They also do theology in order to become more critically aware of their privilege and their responsibility in relation to the poor women in their communities. These middle-class, educated Asian women theologians are learning how to work with poor women and how to be transformed by the wisdom of the poor through the process of doing theology. Asian women theologians know that this process of *metanoia* to poor women is the only way to regain their wholeness.[77]

One aim of Asian feminist theologians is solidarity with poor women. As Asian women theologians connect with the poor and movements for nationalism and against poverty and oppression, "when there is genuine sharing, hearing, and naming for the survival and liberation of the community, *then the community becomes the theologian*."[78] As Chung's and Asian women's theologies strive to locate the voice of theology in the liberation community, Ada María Isasi-Díaz and Yolanda Tarango embody a similar methodological principle in *Hispanic Women: Prophetic Voice in the Church*, where the voices of Hispanic women provide the content and starting point of *mujerista* theology.[79]

ISSUES FOR A COSMOLOGY

Although there are tensions between feminist and womanist theories and theologies, there are analogous goals. One common goal is confrontation of violence, oppression, and exploitation which impact women and women's communities. Another common goal is actualization of women's power, voice, being, relationality, and action. A further shared goal is transformation, revolution, or metamorphosis. However diverse the expressions of these goals, they suggest common ground for women's friendships, solidarity, and coalitions. Unfortunately, the commonalities that promise sisterhood create tensions when sociohistorical contexts and differences are ignored or poorly negotiated.

One set of tensions arises from analysis of patriarchy. Prior to examining the tensions, the value and importance of white feminist analysis of patriarchy should be admitted. In particular, lesbian feminist theology provides a pioneering critical perspective on the role of patriarchy in devaluing and rupturing women's sexual and nonsexual relationships with women. Womanist Delores Williams, in her critique of the limitations of white women's analysis of patriarchy for African-American women, does not discourage white women from defining how patriarchy governs white women's relationships.[80] Within the confines of Euro-American women's experience, analysis of patriarchy is useful and appropriate for exploring the social context of women's oppression. For Euro-American women, analysis of patriarchy is a logical accompaniment to defining separatism, that is, women's dissociation from patriarchy. Tensions arise, however, when Euro-American feminists mistake their experience for the universal experience of women either because of unfamiliarity with the plurality of women's experiences or because of supremacist and/or essentialist implications that white women's experience is fundamental, each cause rendering invisible the experiences of women of color. Tensions are exacerbated by the implication that dissection of gender issues through critique of patriarchy, even when race and class issues among women are considered, is adequate apart from cognizance that Euro-American women have been privileged and advantaged by patriarchy (through educational opportunities, for example) sometimes directly at the expense of poor and minority women.[81]

Separatism is an issue that raises another set of tensions. First is the priority that separatism enjoys in different feminist/womanist philosophies and theologies. Daly's and Raymond's perspectives suggest that feminist separatism is important but clearly subordinate to the centrality of Be-Friending and Gyn/affection. Womanist perspectives, on the other hand, refer to separatism rather incidentally, concurring with Walker's definition that a womanist is not a separatist "except periodically, for health."[82] Womanists' universal concern for the survival and wholeness of the entire black community, as well as love and solidarity with men, precludes separatism as the most viable strategy for survival and revolution in all sociohistorical contexts. Although white feminists and womanists agree that sexism threatens women, separatism is not necessarily a common strategy for confronting sexism. If the implication by Euro-American feminists is that separatism is a mark of feminism, then nonwhite women's experience and commitment to community solidarity are excluded.

Among Euro-American feminists who advocate separatism, there are differences that precipitate a second tension, although admittedly this tension is more an intellectual difference than a threat to collaboration among Daly, Raymond, and Hunt. This tension concerns the difference between personal separatism and worldly or political separatism. Daly claims priority for personal separatism before political separatism. Paring away layers of patriarchal alienation and false selves from the Self is primary in Daly's feminist philosophy but political separatism from or within groups is derivative. Continuous with, but distinct from Daly's position on separatism, Raymond advocates worldly, political separatism that intends to change the world. Worldly separatism creates a context for political empowerment of female friendship even as it nurtures personal integrity. Separatism as segregation or dissociation from the world undermines Gyn/affection—female friendship that has political consequences. Similarly, Hunt is proactive about justice-seeking friendships as political activism. Hunt rejects heterosexual coupling and marriage as paradigms for Christian values in favor of a paradigm based on justice-seeking friendship. Justice-seeking female friendship functions as a standpoint for critical reflection on Christian ethics, including paradigms of female-male relationships. Justice-seeking friends, female friendships, provide a model for both ecological and social ethics, yet Hunt self-critically cautions that the model may not be transferable to different gender, race, class, and cultural contexts and friendships. Hunt's theology is not concerned with separatism but advocates a diverse range of justice-seeking friendships, preeminently the relationship of female friendship as the experiential grounding for a theory of justice-seeking friendship.

The intellectual tension between foregrounding personal separatism and foregrounding political separatism in white feminist theology should continue to be discussed especially in light of solidarity with womanists and feminists of color. If Euro-American feminism insists on prioritizing personal or political separatism, then priorities should be set in light of bell hooks's conditions for solidarity: radical efforts toward eliminating racism, respecting and knowing differences, redistributing wealth, and adopting collective concerns. As Raymond claims, worldlessness generates friendlessness. If white feminists desire solidarity with women of color, then political activism and justice-seeking are part of commitment to that female friendship or coalition. Another way of stating the tension is to say that separatism and solidarity are approached differently, either ontologically (the starting point with the Self) or axiologically (the starting point with activism). The weight of scholarship seems to support an axiological approach to satisfy the demands of diverse women's experiences. However, the question remains whether it is a false dichotomy to oppose personal and political separatism if ontology and axiology are, in fact, concurrent rather than sequential.

Although Daly is correct that not all women can be friends, I contend that solidarity could be actualized more effectively among diverse women than feminist/womanist separation has allowed. White feminist theory has inadvertently (and sometimes intentionally) elected separatism from women of color. White feminism has accomplished separatism from women of color by universalizing white women's experience and by demarcations of white women's experience which abdicates responsibility for relationships with women of color, as in "I write as white, Christian, middle-class, educated, U.S. feminist." Both universalizing and demarcation pretend that womanist experience and feminist/womanist race relations are invisible. Feminist-womanist solidarity is unlikely without a relational feminist theory that supersedes a controlling, self-imposed separatism. If white feminism becomes self-critical, responsible, and proactive, feminist-womanist coalitions are possible. Then reciprocally and mutually, feminists and womanists can define solidarity dialogically. There is promise in exploring how Third World praxis, defined as confluence of reflection and action, can inform feminist separatism as simultaneously personal and political, in comparing whether womanist resistance is analogous to paring away false selves from the Self, and in shaping Be-Friending, Gyn/affection, and sisterhood toward community-based, ecological activism.

My thesis is that Whiteheadian philosophy complements feminist theory. Whiteheadian philosophy and theology are no substitute for original, creative feminist thought, and Whiteheadian philosophy should not be misunderstood as essentialist, foundationalist, or universal for either feminists or

Whiteheadians (and certainly not for womanists), but Whiteheadian philosophy has been helpful to me and other process feminists in providing a useful, coherent relational epistemology. Whitehead's relational philosophy functions for me as a practical interpretive device, assisting me in translating feminist tensions and womanist critiques. The remainder of this chapter is an experiment in interpretation. A Whiteheadian feminist relational philosophy can add a description of women's relationships to those already reviewed in this chapter. Further, Whiteheadian feminist thought can provide a rationale for activism that supports coalitions among feminists and womanists.

FEMALE FRIENDSHIP AS JUDGMENT

Female friendship, Be-Friending, Gyn/affection, justice-seeking friends, sisterhood, and solidarity lend themselves to interpretation from a Whiteheadian feminist perspective. Although I in no way wish to say that feminist, *mujerista*, or womanist views need validation from a "dead, white male philosopher," I do believe, first, that Whiteheadian philosophy will be enhanced by the incorporation of women's experience (inclusive of women's philosophy and theology as part of women's experience). Second, feminist theorists involved in critical and constructive projects ought to become involved in collaborative efforts to express feminist concerns. Multiple modes of expression can only enhance the clarity of feminist constructions. Just as womanist, *mujerista*, and feminist perspectives enhance and support each other, a Whiteheadian feminist understanding may complement and enhance the discussion of women's relationships and separatism. To this end, I want to suggest some Whiteheadian interpretations of feminist separatism and female friendship.

The first point that I wish to make, as a Whiteheadian feminist, is that female friendship may function as a standpoint from which we exercise judgment on hetero-reality and systems of oppression. In Whitehead's philosophy, an operation of judgment may accompany particular perceptions (for example, "perceiving this stone as not grey" or "perceiving this stone as grey"). Whitehead noted that the most general case of conscious perception, the most primitive form of judgment, is the negative perception ("perceiving this stone as not grey"). As Whitehead describes the negative perception in relationship to consciousness, he says,

> Consciousness is the feeling of negation: in the perception of "the stone as grey," such feeling is in barest germ; in the perception of "the stone as not grey," such feeling is in full development. Thus the negative perception is the triumph of consciousness. It finally rises to the peak of free imagination, in which the conceptual novelties search through a universe in which they are not datively exemplified.[83]

We may use this insight to suggest that women have come to consciousness in a most basic way when we become aware of particular negative perceptions. Namely, reality is not hetero-reality, privilege, or supremacy. The universe through which women search imaginatively includes diverse women's experience. In this case, it need not be exclusively the universe of women's experience. If we search through any universe that includes women's experience as we know it, we find that hetero-reality and systems of oppression are not reality in fact. Women have a standpoint from which we make this judgment, from which we experience negative perception of misogynist systems that exploit and oppress. This standpoint is the context of female friendship. Out of this context, we know that hetero-reality is invalidated. It is through female friendship that women have come to consciousness of the pseudoreality of hetero-reality and intersecting forms of oppression. Separatism is the way that some women extricate themselves from pseudoreality, in Raymond's language. We could say that separatism is a judgment, a negative perception of hetero-reality that arises as a consequence of women's friendships and as a form of activism.

Womanists and *mujeristas* in the United States and Third World women globally participate in sisterhood and solidarity that likewise function as judgment, in the Whiteheadian sense. The experiences generated in minority women's relationships in the United States and among Third World women in solidarity deny that white feminist depictions of women's experience completely and accurately reflect the collective experience of women. The diverse standpoints of women invalidate essentialist views of women and expose what could be called "feminist misogyny," the racist, supremacist, and elitist rejection of the plurality of women's experience. Womanist judgment is a negative perception of limited feminist perspectives on the nature of women's reality.

FEMALE FRIENDSHIP AS PROPOSITION

A second feature of Whitehead's philosophy may be used to suggest the propositional character of female friendship and solidarity. A proposition is a lure for feeling. When a proposition is nonconformal, it proposes an alternative potentiality in response to actual lived experience. Such a proposition suggests a novel response to the given world. As Whitehead notes,

> The novelty may promote or destroy order; it may be good or bad. But it is new, a new type of individual, and not merely a new intensity of individual feeling. That member of the locus has introduced a new form into the actual world; or, at least, an old form in a new function.[84]

I want to point out, for example, that Daly's Be-Friending functions as a proposition in several respects. Be-Friending reflects a connection between actuality and potentiality. The actual world within which women function includes deep memory of female connectedness, but it also includes a predominantly hetero-relational mode of female relationships. Be-Friending introduces an alternative potential in response to the world. It would be fair to say that women have not fully separated themselves from hetero-reality. Be-Friending then is largely a potentiality rather than an actuality. As a potential, Be-Friending functions to lure women toward novelty, novelty rooted in actuality. The proposition Be-Friending, when it is admitted into feeling, introduces a new form into the world—"A novelty has emerged into creation."[85]

Womanist literature, theory, and theology suggest that African-American women's sisterhood evokes novelty and, therefore, functions as a locus for the lure for feeling or proposition. In *The Color Purple*, Alice Walker's character Celie emerges from a tragic, abused life into new selfhood because of her friendship with Shug and Sofia. Celie's new possibilities—emergent sexuality, creative work, courageous confrontation of Mr. _____, expansive relationship with God—develop in response to Shug's and Sofia's encouragement and challenge. Othermother relationships, as Collins observes them, are perhaps another example of relationships that partake of a propositional character. Othermothers support children and mothers in the community, but othermother relationships are also visionary relationships that stimulate self-reliance, imaginative goals that defy stereotypes, and strategies for political action and survival. Williams's womanist theology provides a further example of the function of propositions in African-American women's relationships with God. In Williams's theology, God is not primarily Liberator, as in black liberation theologies, but God "who makes a way out of no way," pointing Sarah's slave, Hagar, and black women toward resources that enable them to survive. God points the way, but black women respond to God's lure toward survival by enacting possibilities.

Solidarity is another locus for propositions. When Asian feminist Chung writes about solidarity between educated women theologians and poor women, she refers to the transformation and *metanoia* that are possible for theologians who respond to the wisdom of the poor. Thus, the relationships between educated and poor Asian women embody novelty, possibility, and transformation. Similarly, the challenge to solidarity that Asian feminists, along with *mujerista* and womanist scholars in the United States and the Third World, raise in their critique of Euro-American feminists is a lure toward novel possibilities that promise new forms of feminism.

INTERNAL RELATIONS

Whitehead's doctrine of internal relations may be particularly helpful in interpreting separatism and female friendship. Because the doctrine of internal relations is foundational to process philosophy, we can imagine several levels at which this doctrine makes contact with feminist theory. First, it merely reiterates Daly's maxim that everything that IS is connected with everything else that IS. The pervasive interconnection of all that exists is prevalent in both Whiteheadian and feminist thought. Second, I perceive that Whitehead generally wished to communicate bolder claims about that interconnection than feminists ordinarily assert (unless Daly's reference to the metaphor of the hologram may be understood to suggest something like Whitehead's doctrine of internal relations). Whitehead was suggesting more than the mere fact that we exist as individuals who are connected with other individuals. We are not first individuals who then have relationships. We are not individuals apart from our relationships. In other words, individuals are constituted by relationships. In the process of self-creation, we exist by virtue of our relationships. This means that relationships form the self through their causal efficacy (in a Whiteheadian sense).

I want to suggest how the doctrine of internal relations may enhance an understanding of separatism and female friendship. In the first place, it helps to underscore Raymond's point that the assumptions of hetero-reality are ludicrous. The assumptions that women are not really related to other women and should not be related to other women because women are primarily responsible for sustaining hetero-relations mean that men determine all human relations. These assumptions entail a limited understanding of men and women in relationships, as well as a refusal to imagine the complexity of relationships involving diverse individuals and a multifarious environment. The refusal to acknowledge the homo-relational basis of hetero-reality is a further oversimplification of relationships that reduces the nature of male relationships to specific "acceptable" spheres—male "relationships" involving power struggles among independent, asexual, competitive individuals. The predominant ignore-ance of connectedness with nature is an additional narrowness of relational perception in hetero-reality. All attest to the relational naivete of hetero-reality in comparison with a worldview based on internal relations.

I will note here that Catherine Keller's analysis of patriarchy in terms of the separate selfhood of men and the soluble selfhood of women corroborates the stunted character of relations within the dominant patriarchal worldview, which diminishes both relationality and individuality with its dualistic patterning of subject/object in male/female relationships. The soluble self, typically the female, is a self totally defined in terms of relationships.

The soluble self is literally dissolved in relationships. Her love limits her relationships to the domestic sphere, the maintenance of relationships with husband and children. The soluble self has no genuine self.[86] The separate self, typically the male, exists in independence and opposition. The separate self is apparently absolute and transcendent, because the separate self denies relationships through isolation.[87] Keller helpfully describes internal relations as "in-fluence," flowing in.

> If the other enters my experience, then it enters as an influence upon me: it makes a difference, and so I am no longer quite the same. But influence, to be more precise, is not working *upon* me so much as *into* me; influence is that which flows in. If the other flows into the self, then the other is immanent to the self, to the inside being of that self. This is the philosophical meaning of internal rather than external relations: relations between different subjects that are internal to what those subjects *are*— part of their very essence, for good or for ill.[88]

The separate self experiences relationships as external, refusing to allow relationships the immanence of internal relations. The soluble self complements the separate self in that she is the dependent Other whose internal relations particularly involve the in-fluence of the male in her experience. The soluble self is, thus, constituted by her male-defined relationship(s).

Second, the doctrine of internal relations may be used to interpret the significance of female friendship. If radical feminist separatism, according to Daly, is primarily for the purpose of dis-covering woman's Self and women's Selves in relationship, then the doctrine of internal relations may suggest in part how that happens. According to Whitehead, there is a reciprocal relationship between individuality and society. We become individuals through our social relationships, and we also contribute to society by our completion as individuals. Technically, this is what Whitehead means by creativity. In a context of female friendship, women contribute to my search for my Self, just as the emergence of my Self enhances the metamorphic movement of Gyn/affectionate women. In hetero-reality, the richest contributions to my emergence, the contributions from Gyn/affectionate women, are truncated by an imposed dissociation from female relationships. At the same time, my creative contributions to female friendship are limited, if not eliminated. A doctrine of internal relations indicates just how formative of individual female selfhood female friendship is. It also highlights the contagion of female friendship.

In the third place, the doctrine of internal relations emphasizes the magnitude of the task of separatism and the potential for change which may result from separatism. Because women have participated in hetero-relations, all women need to acknowledge that to a significant extent we are formed by those relationships. Although no woman is a self *determined* by hetero-relations, no woman is free from the powerful influence of hetero-relations in her self-formation. These hetero-relational influences are subtle, pervasive, and deeply ingrained in women's selfhood—feminists who have begun the process of identifying these characteristics in themselves realize that it is a difficult and painful task to be self-critical about hetero-relations. This underscores the reason that separatism is primarily concerned with women's self-formation and female friendships rather than male-female relationships. Sorting out the detrimental hetero-relational components of our own lives is logically prior to a concern for changing hetero-relations in general, because until we have identified the oppression that exists in us, the task of confronting hetero-reality and proposing alternatives will be unfocused. If this interpretation of separatism is reasonable, then feminist separatism may be similar to African-American women's acts of resistance that dignify personal integrity and defy internalized oppression and racism. Further, because this depiction of separatism admits that it is difficult for Euro-American women to identify consciously how we have internalized sexism and feminine stereotypes, it may also provide a model for understanding how Euro-American women have internalized systems of racist, classist, heterosexist, and religious oppression. Transformation of Self, for Anglo feminists, requires confronting the internalized sexism that limits Self and the internalized interlocking systems of oppression that make privileged white women simultaneously the oppressor self and the oppressed self, both beneficiary and victim of oppression. The personal and political are truly inseparable, because separatism circumscribes the political within a set of personal, existential issues.

CAUSAL EFFICACY

In a sense, I refer to an intricate assemblage of Whitehead's concepts when I introduce the topic of internal relations. Especially with respect to political activism and separatism, I want to mention the importance of causal efficacy in internal relations. Causal efficacy is not to be understood in the sense of causal determination of the present as a direct consequence of a linear connection with events in the past. It is more accurate to think of causal efficacy as a mode of perception in the present. The emerging subject in the present moment responds with a measure of freedom to events in its relevant past. The emerging subject determines how it will take account of these influences from its past actual world and to what extent it will be constituted in the present by these relationships. Although the subject has freedom with respect to these relations, it is also the case that each subject has none other than its own actual world as an influence. The narrowness or inclusiveness of that actual world may limit or expand the potential which may be realized by the subject in the present.

Hetero-relations or patriarchy, the world experienced by contemporary women, has had a limiting effect on women. The causal efficacy of women's past on the self-formation of women in the present places tremendous pressure on women to choose male-defined roles and male-directed purposes dictated by the historical force of patriarchal social relations. Although patriarchal history is not deterministic, the past is powerful and difficult to overcome. As long as the past controls the present, women are restricted to trivial existence.

How then may we explain the fact that women are finding a wider range of options open to them? In part, it is because women are dis-covering a past that was obscured by hetero-relations. Women are less inclined to repeat the hetero-relational past and more inspired to make choices opened by "herstory." Historians, such as Gerda Lerner, are recovering the lost chapters of women's history, that is, both the celebrations of women's achievements and the tragedy of race and class betrayal, and exposing patriarchal biases in the interpretation of history as it has been given to us. The literature of women is being recovered with renewed interest—the novels of Zora Neale Hurston are once again available due to the efforts of Alice Walker and others. This new historical information creates different options for women. Janice Raymond's historical methodology uncovers in the separatist communities of the convent and the Chinese antimarriage sect new options for Gyn/affection and female friendship. In part, we also owe the discovery of women's freedom credit for increasing women's options. Women are not limited to hetero-relational choices; we are not determined by a patriarchal past. The hazardous discovery that women have freedom of choice means that women risk living out of new alternatives, hoping that the rewards of richer experience will outweigh negative consequences.

As women deviate from hetero-relational and patriarchal norms, feminists must be concerned with whether we are involved with private rebellions or whether personal change has efficacy for the transformation of hetero-relations. As I reflect on the potential that radical feminist separatism has for change (the introduction of novel forms) into social, political, and economic relationships, I must agree with Raymond that the intentional political dissociation of women is a form of separatism with limited efficacy and with hooks that white feminism has focused too long on victimization. Worldless dissociation of women is, in effect, segregation of women. Not only is this a silencing of women by hetero-reality, but it is an elimination of women's influence in the world and a betrayal of women who need solidarity and political coalition. On the other hand, worldly dissociation of women from hetero-reality may expand the dimensions of the world, multiplying creative options for the future. Ultimately, the bold immersion of Gyn/affectionate power and potential into a wide range of contexts in confrontation of *all* forms of oppression is the only way to assure historical contributions of female friendship to the actual world.

FEMALE FRIENDSHIP AS CONTRAST

The introduction of female friendship into a largely hetero-relational world makes visible the complexity of the world. Gyn/affectionate power makes women and men uncomfortable, because it shatters an oversimplified view of reality and forces us to reconsider our hetero-relational perspective. Female friendship inspires the process of personal self-formation and reintegration in light of the introduction of a Gyn/affectionate anomaly into our experience.

Whitehead's notion of contrast may inform an analysis of the impact of female friendship on hetero-relations. Contrast describes the mode by which we deal with the complex of entities or events in our actual world. Consciously we may experience this complexity by attempting to make sense of new sensa or information—we integrate the new phenomena into our perception of reality. Whitehead describes how we take account of complexity in a much more fundamental way through contrast. Because each person is herself an experiencing subject, she is ever in the process of "feeling" or "prehending" a wealth of phenomena that will fund her self-formation in each new moment. For the human person, this may entail an overwhelming and diverse range of influences. The problem, which we normally manage easily and even unconsciously, is how this vast quantity of data may be unified within our current experience. According to Whitehead, we manage to prehend the multiplicity by means of contrast, the unity of complex data. Contrast, one of the existents in Whitehead's categoreal scheme, is a mode of synthesis of entities in one prehension, which he calls patterned entities.[89] Contrasts make possible the unity of diversity within experiences. The harmony of contrasts permits us to include complexity, which results in intensity of experience, in our self-formation. The feeling that we have of our world is given depth by contrasts, rather than reducing the complexity to triviality. "Contrast elicits depth, and only shallow experience is possible when there is a lack of patterned contrast."[90] Feeling complexity as contrasts, instead of dismissing (or negatively prehending) complexities as anomalies or incompatibilities, intensifies experience.[91]

Whitehead's philosophy explains the limiting consequences that result when contrasts do not enter into experience.[92] We may use this feature of Whitehead's thought to describe the consequences of hetero-relations, particularly with regard to women's experience. Generally speaking, we may say that women's experience has been relegated to the background of experience which informs society and individuals. On one hand, women's experience is trivialized. Women's experience is recognized but attributed little importance. Women's experience is distinct as a matter of incompatible differentiation. Instead of being entertained as a contrast, women's experience is assigned little relative value in the world of experiences. At extremes, women's experience may even be eliminated as an influence on the emerging world. On the other hand, women's experience may be homogenized with other experiences. Its differences may be seen as irrelevant. In this case, women's experience is undervalued by excessive identification of women's experience with hetero-relations. Analogously, racism, classism, and heterosexism (interlocking systems of oppression) trivialize and homogenize women's experiences at the hands of both privileged men and women. There is lack of discrimination about the distinct character of women's experience and diverse women's experiences. The consequences for individual and social creativity are seriously limited by the failure to include women's experience with intensity of feeling and with discrimination as part of the complexity of the universe. The undervaluing of women's experience truncates the level and intensity of experience which may be actualized.

Female friendship argues the case that women's experience is creative. The marginalization and the elimination of women's literature, history, and ideas have diminished women's Selves, women's community, and our worldviews. Through separatism, women have discovered for themselves and for their communities that Gyn/affection is a key to richer experience.

The impact of feminist movement since the 1960s has motivated women to reconsider their identities. Each woman is faced with more complex choices about her life than the 1950s permitted. The writings of de Beauvoir, Friedan, Greer, and Steinem awakened Euro-American woman's critical eye and directed its scrutiny to her Self and her relationships. The suggestion that a woman has rights regarding her own body and choices about contraception and abortion forced individual women to consider responsible choices about their bodies, their futures, their relationships. Confronted with new alternatives—a married woman keeping her own name, women entering traditionally male professions, a minister preaching sermons with inclusive language, a voter supporting lesbian and gay marriage, a privileged woman witnessing discrimination against women of color in the work place, a U.S. consumer responding to exploitation of Latin American and Asian laborers—each woman faces both practical and ideological questions for herself. The alternatives may be dismissed. The complexity may lead to vagueness or to confusion. Brought into immediate focus as lively contrasts, however, this complexity is a creative stimulus for female selfhood.

Contrast is creative for female friendship, because it allows diverse women to form unique communities. As surely as the complex world emerging from feminist perspectives has challenged the individual woman to re-create herself or to create herself differently, it has also stimulated women to imagine new styles of woman-woman relating. Entertaining contrasts, women address hierarchical and separatist issues as aspects of female friendship. The creativity that contrasts engender has led women to embrace their diversity rather than to establish conformity. There is respect and even excitement in realizing and expressing the differences among women.[93] Seeing the distinction between the experiences of black and white women, for example, has been creative for feminist movement, because it resulted from womanist perspectives voiced by African-American women. These differences do not destroy the solidarity of women; they expand the dimensions and intensity of female friendship.

The Gyn/affectionate power of female friendship need not be limited to the transformations that it may effect in women and women's relationships. Female friendship is just as surely a change agent in the extended community, for male selfhood and hetero-relational society have been equally diminished by the elimination of women's experience from the culture and may justifiably be confronted with its distinctive contributions. The separatist woman and female friendship ultimately present a curiosity to hetero-relational society and may be considered a contrast. When female friendships entertain diverse women's experiences as contrasts, creative and constructive alternatives for social, political, economic, and ecological relations flower. The magnitude of female friendship as a political power is not easily dismissed as an irrelevant incompatibility, and it is less and less likely to be co-opted into hetero-relations. Women's concerns have affected the publishing industry with respect to inclusive language, the insurance industry and the work place with respect to maternity benefits, and to some extent the legal system with regard to sexism and violence against women. Separatism that presents a worldly contrast to hetero-relations demands creative change.

SEPARATISM, SELF, AND SOCIETY

To some extent, separatism as a private affair for some women and women's communities provides a retreat from hetero-relations for the purpose of sorting out which of our patterns of behavior, attitudes, and ideas are fashioned by hetero-relations. Separatism provides a perspective from which women examine themselves for constituents that are self-betrayals and for characteristics that are genuine to ourselves. It is a context for imagination—because we have little history and few models, separatism is a place for self-creation and a safe house for experimentation with selfhood.

Separatism allows a true Self to precipitate out of soluble selfhood when women have reached a saturation point with hetero-relations. Hetero-relations relegate a woman's relationships to those that sustain male-defined hetero-reality. The soluble self so immerses herself in relationships that her selfhood literally dissolves in the work of dependence and sustenance of the male separate self. Separatism is the process whereby woman recovers herself and redefines herself with respect to her relationality. Separatism is the context within which woman becomes more fully herself and consequently more genuinely relational. Recalling Bernard Loomer, we may apply his description of size to the concept of separatism: "the volume of life you can take into your being and still maintain your integrity and individuality, the intensity and variety of outlook you can entertain in the unity of your being without feeling defensive or insecure."[94] Loomer's concept of size describes one who is truly a Self, one who has integrity, individuality, and unity of being. This is not one who is so immersed in relationships that selfhood is obscured and personal identity becomes blurred. It is not, on the other hand, a separate and nonrelational personhood. A person of size has a solid, confident identity that is open to relationships that involve range and diversity. Separatism is the process by which women come to know themselves as persons of integrity who are open to relationships without being reduced to their relationships.

As a social process, separatism functions to create female friendship. Separatism permits women to end the self-loathing that limits relationships with other women. Women's self-hate is expressed in alienation from other women. Separatism is a spiraling of selfhood and sisterhood. Women need female friendship to inspire the discovery of Self. A woman who has discovered her selfhood contributes to female friendship. Woman contributes something of herself to sisterhood and solidarity, and female friendship is formative of woman's Self. There is interdependence and independence between individual women and sisterhood. Continuing Loomer's description of size, we see that size is "the strength of your spirit to encourage others to become freer in the development of their diversity and uniqueness."[95] This unity of purpose within female friendship, sisterhood, and solidarity expresses the Gyn/affection of women's Selves for each other.

The primary purpose of separatism is the flowering of female selfhood and female friendship, and when limited to this particular context, separatism is transformative for women. The issue is whether separatism is as fully transforming of women's experience when it is a worldless separatism. Worldless separatism may not be as far-reaching as worldly separatism for two reasons. In the first place, worldless separatism is a ghettoization of women that limits the range and diversity of experience with which women may interact. Granted, much of that experience will involve confrontation with hetero-relations, but even that involvement is a stimulus for growth as long as women maintain a separatist perspective. Unfortunately, worldless separatism may risk unnecessary separation of women from each other. Limiting the diversity of women in relationship with each other narrows the focus of feminist concerns. Worldless separatism threatens global solidarity of women and abandons excluded women to multiple jeopardy and interlocking systems of domination. In the second place, worldless separatism may be a disservice to the liberation of women when the impact of Gyn/affectionate power is indirect. Worldless separatism allows institutions to remain unaffected by female power. Worldly separatism, on the other hand, empowers women within the spheres of politics, education, economics, and culture. The direct impact of Gyn/affection on hetero-relations has the power to transform oppressive structures. Worldly separatism enlarges the environment within which women may discover themselves and other female Selves. As worldly separatists, women acknowledge the full range of relationships within which women are engaged—whether those relationships are female friendships, local or family communities, or oppressive relationships, worldly separatists participate in a multiplicity of relationships with a commitment to enriching women's Selves, female friendship, and women's coalitions.

NOTES

1. Much earlier consideration of topics in this chapter appeared in *Process Studies* 18, no. 2: 78–87, in an article entitled "Radical Relatedness and Feminist Separatism." In this chapter, the work on separatism, Mary Daly, and Janice Raymond relies on this earlier publication.
2. Mary Daly, in cahoots with Jane Caputi, *Websters' First New Intergalactic Wickedary of the English Language* (Boston: Beacon Press, 1987), 96.
3. Mary Daly, *Gyn/Ecology: The Metaethics of Radical Feminism* (Boston: Beacon Press, 1978), 381.
4. Mary Daly, *Pure Lust: Elemental Feminist Philosophy* (Boston: Beacon Press, 1978), 362.
5. Ibid.
6. Daly, *Gyn/Ecology*, 382.
7. Ibid., 382–83.
8. Daly, *Pure Lust*, 362.
9. Ibid., 373.
10. Ibid., 375.
11. Daly, *Gyn/Ecology*, 319.
12. Ibid., 367.
13. Ibid., 370.
14. Ibid., 371–73.
15. Ibid., 26.
16. Daly, *Pure Lust*, 248.
17. Ibid., 374.
18. Ibid., 386.
19. Janice G. Raymond, *A Passion for Friends: Toward a Philosophy of Female Affection* (Boston: Beacon Press, 1986), 3. Raymond illustrates the phenomenon

of perceiving women together as women alone by example. Women together at a bar are asked why they are alone, because they are without the companionship of men. Women together in restaurants are not waited on as readily, because they are not perceived in the same way as women in the company of men.

20. Ibid., 41–42.
21. Ibid., 144.
22. Ibid., 153.
23. Ibid., 152.
24. Ibid., 153.
25. Ibid., 232.
26. Ibid., 253.
27. Ibid., 232.
28. Mary E. Hunt, *Fierce Tenderness: A Feminist Theology of Friendship* (New York: Crossroad, 1991).
29. Ibid., 29.
30. Ibid., 80–84.
31. Ibid., 99.
32. Ibid., 100.
33. Ibid., 101.
34. Ibid., 102.
35. Ibid., 105.
36. Ibid., 106–8.
37. Ibid., 146–47.
38. Ibid., 171.
39. Ibid., 173.
40. Ibid., 175.
41. Ibid., 114.
42. Zora Neale Hurston, *Their Eyes Were Watching God* (Urbana and Chicago: University of Illinois Press, 1978), 29.
43. Ibid., 17.
44. Ibid., 161, 192.
45. Ntozake Shange, *Sassafrass, Cypress, and Indigo* (New York: St. Martin's Press, 1982).
46. Patricia Hill Collins, *Black Feminist Thought: Knowledge, Consciousness, and the Politics of Empowerment* (New York: Routledge, 1991), 96.
47. Ibid., 96–97.
48. Ibid., 131.
49. Ibid.
50. Ibid., 129.
51. Ibid., 97.
52. Alice Walker, *In Search of Our Mothers' Gardens* (New York: Harcourt, Brace, Jovanovich, 1983), xi. Cited in Collins, *Black Feminist Thought*, 38.
53. Collins, *Black Feminist Thought*, 38.
54. bell hooks, *Feminist Theory: From Margin to Center* (Boston: South End Press, 1984), 45.
55. Angela Davis, *Women, Race and Class* (New York: Random House; Vintage Books, 1983).
56. Jacquelyn Grant, *White Women's Christ and Black Women's Jesus: Feminist Christology and Womanist Response* (Atlanta, Ga.: Scholars Press, 1989), 195, 200.

57. Delores S. Williams, *Sisters in the Wilderness: The Challenge of Womanist God-Talk* (Maryknoll, N.Y.: Orbis Books, 1993), 184. Kelly Brown Douglas, *The Black Christ* (Maryknoll, N.Y.: Orbis Books, 1994), 95.
58. hooks, *Feminist Theory*, 54–62.
59. Ibid., 65.
60. Ibid., 64.
61. Judith Plaskow, "Appropriation, Reciprocity, and Issues of Power," *Journal of Feminist Studies in Religion* 8, no. 2 (Fall 1992): 106–7.
62. Kwok Pui-lan, "Speaking from the Margins," *Journal of Feminist Studies in Religion* 8, no. 2 (Fall 1992): 103.
63. Ada María Isasi-Díaz, "Viva la Diferencia!" *Journal of Feminist Studies in Religion* 8, no. 2 (Fall 1992): 99.
64. Ibid., 100.
65. Ibid. Toinette M. Eugene, "On 'Difference' and the Dream of Pluralistic Feminism," *Journal of Feminist Studies in Religion* 8, no. 2 (Fall 1992): 98.
66. Walker, *In Search of Our Mothers' Gardens*, xi.
67. Douglas, *The Black Christ*, 98–99.
68. Ibid., 105.
69. Williams, *Sisters in the Wilderness*, xiv.
70. Ibid., 185.
71. Ibid., xiv.
72. Chung Hyun Kyung, *Struggle to Be the Sun Again: Introducing Asian Women's Theology* (Maryknoll, N.Y.: Orbis Books, 1990), 35.
73. Ibid., 27.
74. Ibid., 54.
75. Douglas, *The Black Christ*, 102–3.
76. Ibid., 114.
77. Chung, *Struggle to Be the Sun Again*, 102.
78. Ibid., 103.
79. Ada María Isasi-Díaz and Yolanda Tarango, *Hispanic Women: Prophetic Voice in the Church* (Minneapolis: Fortress Press, 1992), xiv–xv.
80. Williams, *Sisters in the Wilderness*, 186.
81. Ibid.
82. Walker, *In Search of Our Mothers' Gardens*, xi.
83. Whitehead, *Process and Reality*, 161.
84. Ibid., 187.
85. Ibid.
86. Catherine Keller, *From a Broken Web: Separation, Sexism, and Self* (Boston: Beacon Press, 1986), 17.
87. Ibid., 26.
88. Ibid., 27.
89. Whitehead, *Process and Reality*, 22.
90. Ibid., 114.
91. Ibid., 83.
92. I refer to Whitehead's discussion of satisfaction in *Process and Reality*. See especially pages 111 and 166.
93. Linda J. "Tess" Tessier refers to this phenomenon in female friendship as "reverence for differences."
94. Bernard Loomer, "S-I-Z-E," *Criterion* 13 (Spring 1974): 6.
95. Ibid.

RELATING TO GOD

MARY DALY'S BOOK *Beyond God the Father* marked the rising spirit of feminist theology and philosophy of the early 1970s. In the first place, *Beyond God the Father* joined mounting feminist criticism of Christianity. It located sexism in Christian patriarchalism largely in the dominant image of God the Father. Daly advocated castration of the Supreme Phallus, the inadequate God, who is ambiguously characterized as spirit yet male in scholarly conceptualizations.[1] Although Daly's work in this volume was primarily critical, it was not without important constructive elements—its second contribution. Daly focused on the feminist task of liberating language as the methodology for liberation of women. As a significant act of *"castrating* of language and images that reflect and perpetuate the structures of a sexist world," Daly proposed new imagery for the divine—God as Be-ing, the Verb of Verbs, in whom women experience being by participation in being.[2] The legacy of *Beyond God the Father* is further creative imaging of deity by Daly within a creative network of other feminists who are proposing images.

FEMINISM AND GOD

The range of woman-identified imagery for deity is truly diverse. Letty Russell, who is a revisionist advocate of human liberation, draws imagery from a synthesis of Barthian theology, theology of hope, and liberation theology. Russell's understanding of God is based on a Trinitarian image of God-in-action. Russell's imagery is intended to correct an emphasis on patriarchy and male dominance, as well as the hierarchical implications of parent-child metaphors. The Trinity models both liberation and reciprocity. The dynamic presence of God who acts in history is imaged as God the Creator who will bring about the New Creation, God the Liberator who has ushered in freedom in the New Creation, and God the Advocate who continues liberation for the captives.[3] This image of God models partnership for men and women and expresses the dynamic, historic activity of the living God.

In *Sexism and God-Talk*, Rosemary Ruether has attempted to balance feminine and masculine imagery for God in the analytical symbol "God/ess."

With this symbol, Ruether wants to avoid the dominating imagery of king-ship, while maintaining the unity of the Judeo-Christian concept of deity. Ruether argues that the biblical tradition contains liberating imagery for women and that God/ess is an image that is inclusive of women's experience. God/ess images arise from the socially oppressed and should inspire transformation, liberation, and redemption. To enact such possibilities, God/ess must not entail women's experience as a stereotype of female subordination to male dominance. "Adding an image of God/ess as loving, nurturing mother, mediating the power of the strong, sovereign father, is insufficient."[4] God/ess is the creator of full personhood, source of being. God/ess, in this sense, is the antithesis of nature/spirit dualism. It is the *Shalom* or "harmonization of self and body, self and other, self and world."[5] God/ess is the primordial matrix.

Womanist theologian Delores Williams explicitly departs from metaphors of God the Liberator found in black liberation theology and images of God in feminist liberation theologies. Williams's hermeneutic interprets the bib-lical witness in terms of texts that express "God's word of survival and quality of life to oppressed communities (or families) living in a diaspora."[6] The survival/quality-of-life hermeneutic generates imagery for God that dif-fers from God as Liberator.[7] First, Williams quarrels with black liberation theology, particularly James Cone, for the normative claim that God's lib-eration is universal for all oppressed people and for the paradigmatic use of the Hebrew exodus and election.[8] The Genesis accounts of Hagar, the Egyp-tian slave of Sarah, function as Williams's paradigmatic story, and from that story, Williams observes that God did not liberate Hagar and, in fact, privileged Sarah, the slaveholder. Second, Williams differs with feminist lib-eration theology, namely Mexican theologian Elsa Tamez. Tamez reads the Hagar story from the context of liberation movement and interprets God's action toward Hagar as liberating. Reading from African-American women's experience of economic enslavement and ancestral slavery, Williams, on the other hand, heightens awareness that Hagar was not liberated by God in either divine encounter in the wilderness. God provided visions for survival where Hagar had not seen them before—for example, God sided with Sarah by speaking to Abraham and supporting Sarah's request that Hagar and her son Ishmael be expelled from their household, but in the wilderness, God pointed Hagar toward the well that enabled survival in spite of the fact that mother and son were abandoned without food or water.[9] Williams's image of God reflects black women's faith that God is the one who provides new vision for survival. Like Hagar, black Christian women trust that "God helps them make a way out of no way."[10] The immediate experience of Hagar and African-American women is that liberation is dependent on women's action. From the biblical witness that God liberates some, but not all the oppressed, the survival/quality-of-life hermeneutic affirms that "liberation is an ultimate, but in the meantime survival and prosperity must be the experience of our people."[11]

Chung Hyun Kyung's Asian feminist theological "epistemology from the broken body" begins with Asian women's suffering.[12] Because Asian women understand themselves to be made in God's image, theology begins with anthropology in the dual experience of suffering and hope.[13] For Asian women, this epistemology suggests transformative thinking about images of God— God as both female and male, God as the community in relationship, God as Creator in nature and history, God as life-giving Spirit, and God as Mother and Woman. Citing Astrid Lobo, an Indian scientist and Catholic, Chung notes among Asian women a movement from understanding themselves as victims and God as rescuer to recognizing Asian women's strength, power, and resources as the life-giving Spirit of God within them.[14] The image of God as Woman and Mother recognizes Asian women's bodies and woman-hood as valuable, but these images of God also transform the immutable, unchangeable, patriarchal God of tradition. God as Woman and Mother is approachable, personable, and accepting of women.

> This female God is a vulnerable God who is willing to be changed and transformed in her interaction with Asian women in their everyday life experiences. This God is a God who talks to Asian women, listens to their story, and weeps with them. This God is a God who struggles with Asian women in their claims of power in this world, a God who is grow-ing, changing, and walking with them.[15]

The metaphors for God emerging in Asian women's theology picture an inclusive, responsive, relational deity.

Non-Christian women's spirituality informs and creates metaphors for the divine—we may take as an example Starhawk's interpretation of the God-dess from a Wiccan or pagan perspective. Starhawk associates the Goddess with two other important concepts that suggest the significance of the God-dess symbol. First, Goddess expresses the primary concept of power-from-within, which Starhawk contrasts with the predominant interpretation of power-over or domination. Second, Goddess is the normative symbol of immanence. Immanent power is power-from-within. In contrast to estrange-ment, immanence refers to "the awareness of the world and everything in it as alive, dynamic, interdependent, interacting, and infused with moving en-ergies: a living being, a weaving dance."[16] The Goddess images the divine in nature and humans, and this means that the Goddess cannot be limited to a single image. The Goddess is many. History and mythology provide names for a number of these images—from earth to moon and stars to Mother. The images are predominantly female because they are intended to depict the birth of life into the world and the value of the earth. The Goddess conjures in the imagination an idea of connection, creativity, and nurture. Goddess imagery instantly evokes (and invokes) an identification with women's experiences of birth, growth, loving, aging, and dying. This is an identification that is liberating for women, but it is not exclusively female. Starhawk notes that unlike male images of deity, which exclude the female, Goddess imagery is inclusive of male and female. If the Goddess is an affirmation of all that has been given life, it is consequently an affirmation of male and female. The Goddess is the immanence of divinity in the world, the immanence of divinity in women, men, and nature. Invoking the Goddess (as Gaea) connects us to the earth; it grounds us in the power of the Goddess, which becomes power-from-within as we integrate it into ourselves.

The suggestion of a pantheistic interpretation of divinity is not limited to Starhawk or pagan perspectives as such. The value of nature in providing metaphors for God is apparent in a number of feminist sources, including ecofeminism and feminist literature. Alice Walker creates a noteworthy example of a shift from white, male imagery to nature imagery for God in *The Color Purple*. The characters Celie and Shug are involved in a discussion about God and what God looks like. Celie has come to the conclusion that God is like all other men, "trifling, forgitful and lowdown." Shug, in her own way, believes that Celie's despair is more a matter of Celie's perspective on God, which reflects the "white folks' white bible." Shug testifies to her move away from the white folks' God.

> My first step from the old white man was trees. Then air. Then birds. Then other people. But one day when I was sitting quiet and feeling like a motherless child, which I was, it come to me: that feeling of being part of everything, not separate at all. I knew that if I cut a tree, my arm would bleed.[17]

Shug's God is neither male nor female, but an It imaged in nature. The profound revelation is that all things are interconnected in God. For Celie, it doesn't prove to be easy to adopt this new perspective on God, but she takes Shug's advice—"You have to git man off your eyeball, before you can see anything a'tall."

> Man corrupt everything, say Shug. He on your box of grits, in your head, and all over the radio. He try to make you think he everywhere. Soon as you think he everywhere, you think he God. But he ain't. Whenever you trying to pray, and man plop himself on the other end of it, tell him to git lost, say Shug. Conjure up flowers, wind, water, a big rock.[18]

Shug recommends to Celie her way of cleansing herself of patriarchal images of God: Look to nature to find God.

Celie's response summarizes the awesome task before feminists and womanists constructing images for God.

But this hard work, let me tell you. He been there so long, he don't want to budge. He threaten lightening, floods and earthquakes. Us fight. I hardly pray at all. Every time I conjure up a rock, I throw it.[19]

The process of introducing and testing new images for God is difficult. New metaphors are not easily taken into consideration by mainstream religion. God the Father has not budged to accommodate God the Mother. Although many feminists and womanists cited here propose images that are inclusive of female and male aspects, their metaphors are threatening to Christianity. In spite of the conflict and the anger, which accompany the project of reimaging God, feminist/womanist constructive theology must persist in multiplying liberating images.

MCFAGUE'S MODELS OF GOD

In her books *Metaphorical Theology* and *Models of God*, Sallie McFague has addressed the project of creating images for God. Metaphors and models, which are extended metaphors, are the essence of nonconceptual religious language. Metaphors, simply by definition, are words or phrases used out of context. Metaphors are applied inappropriately to an unfamiliar context for the purpose of describing indirectly what cannot be described directly. An obvious example is God the Father. The metaphor "father" is applied in an inappropriate context to express indirectly what we mean by "God." There is no identity between a metaphor and its referent. A metaphor suggests some similarities between the image and a lesser known context, but it is not a definition. Thus, a metaphor is a suggestion of what "is" similar between the image and the referent, but it also entails an "is not" character, which admits indirectness and inappropriateness.[20]

The "is" and "is not" characteristics of metaphor confess that it is impossible for any single metaphor to exhaust the definition or description of that to which it refers. A metaphor is necessarily an incomplete expression. Consequently "God the Father" never expresses fully what we mean by "God." The vast experiences of the Christian God are not entirely contained in the fatherhood of God. Setting feminist concerns aside for the moment, the nature of metaphorical religious language is such that a singular investment in the exclusivist language of God as Father is idolatry. Our only safeguard against idolatry in divine imagery is the multiplication of metaphors for God, each of which contributes its unique and fresh insights into the nature of God.[21]

Models, because of their "staying power," are particularly susceptible to reification and exaggerated, exclusive dominance. This idolatry is especially threatening when we become aware that the model is a dangerous one. McFague argues that this is the case for the monarchical model of God. The model of God as King is dangerous in three respects. First, it images God as distant from the world. God's kingdom is otherworldly. Second, God's concern is primarily for the human creature. The divine relationship is with humans rather than nature. Third, God controls the world through domination and benevolence. The implication of the model is that God acts hierarchically *upon* the world rather than *in* it. The model fails largely because it cannot express "an understanding of the gospel as a destabilizing, inclusive, nonhierarchical vision of fulfillment for all of creation."[22]

McFague proposes that there are three relational models that more adequately image God and the God-world relationship. These three models reflect features that McFague finds essential in contemporary theology: "a sense of our intrinsic interdependence with all forms of life, an inclusive vision that demolishes oppressive hierarchies, accepts responsibility for nurturing and fulfilling life in its many forms, and is open to change and novelty as a given of existence."[23] These three models have in common the presupposition of a prior metaphor, the world as God's body. Thus, all three models are panentheistic. The idea of God's embodiment in the world already proposes certain characteristics of the relationship between God and the world: that God knows the world with immediacy, that God's action in the world is interior, that God loves bodies (which are connected with spirit), and that God feels the suffering of the world.[24]

McFague's three models call on the most essential human relationships as indirect descriptions of God. The first metaphor is God as Mother. McFague associates agapaic love with this model. *Agape* is love which gives life; it is the love instantiated in creation. The creation imaged here is not just birth; it is also nurturing. The relationship of God as Mother with the world is one of interdependence through creation. The second metaphor is God as Lover. *Eros* is the love associated with this model of God. It expresses God's intimate and passionate love for the world. God the Lover finds the world attractive and desires union with the beloved. The relationship of God and the world is responsive. The third metaphor is God as Friend. The *philia* of God images the free choice of friendship, which is a reciprocal relationship. Friendship is inclusive, because anyone can be a friend and because friendships are diverse. This model captures mutuality, commitment, trust, and interdependence as features of the God-world relationship.[25]

McFague's metaphorical theology is noteworthy for a number of reasons. First, it is rooted in a feminist perspective, which rejects exclusively male, hierarchical models of God. Second, it embodies an ecofeminist consciousness. Third, it is a compelling argument for incorporating the shocking models of God as Mother, Lover, and Friend. Fourth, McFague's models introduce an alternative interpretation of omnipotence (derived from process thought) that is persuasive, relational, and mutual. McFague refers to this power as the power of love.

WOMEN AND POWER

Feminists do not seem particularly preoccupied with the topic of divine omnipotence. The issue of prime importance to women is power itself. Feminist thought, whether philosophical or theological, is rooted in women's experience, which we identify largely with the historical experience of women as oppressed. As an oppressed community, women existentially and theoretically focus on power issues as central to women's concerns.

Women perceive that these issues of power and powerlessness are integral to an imposed and inherited patriarchal worldview. This worldview emphasizes individuality and separation. Discrete individuals jockey for power and freedom against each other. This is not a random and chaotic power struggle, but instead it is regimented by particular rules maintained and chosen by those predisposed to be the powerful within patriarchy. A hierarchical value system coupled with a dualistic interpretation of value creates a complex matrix of power relationships, which includes the dualistic separation of male and female and the hierarchical disvaluation of women. Built into patriarchy is the endowment of men with power. By definition, this is "power over" in a hierarchical framework.

Inevitably theism developed within a patriarchal worldview will reflect this dualistic, hierarchical perspective. The metaphors that communicate the man-made image of God are consistent with the basic assumptions of patriarchy. Attributes projected onto God by patriarchy reflect the values of a patriarchal worldview: transcendence (dualistic separation); hierarchical power; possession of maximum freedom, knowledge, territory (omnipresence-infinity), and stability (all of which are masculine values). Perhaps patriarchal theology will admit that these man-made images are metaphors, but rarely is there the admission that this is in fact idolatry. As Sallie McFague has noted about the role of metaphor, when we say "God is the Father" long enough, we begin to believe also that the father/man/male is God. Consequently, we believe that the petty all-controlling power idealized in patriarchal religion is just, good, and divine. A God described by these man-made attributes is irrelevant to women and women's experience. More tragically, this theism institutionalizes the diminishment of women and women's experience. The death of God, therefore, did not leave any grieving widows among feminists.

Feminists and womanists who have not abandoned altogether the project of theism agree with Alice Walker's character Shug that before we can really see God, we have to "git man off our eyeball." We replace this preoccupation with an emphasis on women's experience, especially feminist revision of power, which arises from our dis-covery of the meaning of power in female friendships. The inclination of feminists who reflect on female affection is to write about mutual empowerment rather than oppositional power. One feminist project is the empowerment of Self and female Selves. The empowerment of others is not a project that diminishes one's personal power. Empowered, empowering female friendships provide a context for empowerment of Self. This vision of power is antithetical to hierarchical power. Feminist theologians and thealogians then ask, What new metaphors does this suggest for divinity? Can divine omnipotence be reimagined as empowerment?

ISSUES FOR A COSMOLOGY

Feminist and womanist constructive theology is invested in creating religious language responsive to women's experience of and relationship with God. Although it is common for feminists and womanists to criticize God-talk that is patriarchal or limited to masculine imagery, one of the issues in naming God concerns whether feminist religious language should be female-and-male-inclusive or exclusively woman-centered (but not feminine). Mary Daly's strong talk about castrating language, in her early philosophy, culminated surprisingly in advocating androgynous religious language, but the next phase of Daly's work grew toward gynomorphic, woman-identified, gynocentric Goddess-language that named Be-ing as "a Verb, and that She is many verbs."[26] Starhawk's Goddess and Ruether's God/ess, on the other hand, are inclusive references to deity. McFague's and Chung's inclusive metaphors for God include images of God as Mother, Woman, Friend, and Lover. Russell and Tamez understand God as Liberator inclusively. A second consideration in feminist/womanist God-naming is how to understand God's liberating activity. Russell, Ruether, Tamez, and others construct God-talk in terms of the liberating action of God in history. Williams, on the other hand, is reluctant to interpret God's action primarily as liberation, because the biblical witness attests that not all the oppressed are liberated and that God's action supports women-initiated liberation. At stake are reflections on the power of women to liberate themselves, a more reciprocal empowering relationship between women and God, and the relationships of God's power and action to women's experience. A third issue concerns how retrieval of images for God in religious traditions relates to feminist/womanist theological construction. Williams, for example, retrieves the image of God as Way Maker from African-American religious history. The issue of retrieval concerns discernment about whether historical images of God can be reintroduced in a new historical context without carrying oppressive connotations. A fourth matter of discernment in feminist/womanist God-talk is whether the nature of God should be expressed universally or contextually. Chung, Williams, and Tamez announce the contexts out of which they experience and name God. Ruether and Russell similarly express the need to consider sociohistorical context and situation-variability of God-talk. A fifth concern (and the last that I will address in a field of many more considerations) is the need for a plurality of metaphors to describe God. McFague and Starhawk each emphasize the importance of a multiplicity of images for God in order that diverse God-world relationships may be expressed.

Naming God is supported by particular feminist/womanist theological or philosophical assumptions and observations, one of which is the relational character of God. McFague argues that the root metaphors of Christianity are relational and personal, and in keeping with her tradition, McFague proposes that the metaphors Mother, Lover, and Friend are contemporary models for God, which are inclusive and ecological. Describing God and the God-world relationship, McFague proposes that the world is the body of God and envisions the God-word relationship as panentheistic, immanent without eliminating the transcendent character of the relationship. Chung identifies relationality and immanence as features of Asian feminist theology. Asian women experience God as community in relationship rather than as an individual. The communal model of God advocates mutuality, interdependence, harmony, and growth and empowers women to their rights and responsibilities in community by displacing an image of God as solitary, hierarchical, dominating power.[27] Further, God who is life-giving Spirit is immanent within Asian women and every life-giving thing. Russell relational imagery elects partnership as the lens through which to understand male-female and God-human relationships. Starhawk, too, supports relationality and immanence in a Wiccan pantheistic interpretation of the Goddess. Wiccan images of Goddess play upon the interactive, interdependent, living creativity in nature and humans as divinity. The immanence of Goddess is evident in power-from-within.

A second assumption among some feminists and womanists is that a relational understanding of divinity affects how we conceive the notion of divine power and human empowerment. Asian women's rejection of an individual, all-powerful God for God as community accompanies confidence that this new transformative imagery for God is empowering for Asian women. Starhawk's location of Goddess in the dynamics and interrelationships of the world situates power-from-within all that lives. Williams's womanist interpretation of the biblical witness focuses on God who empowers women to make a way out of no way rather than God who liberates by divine power. How divine power and action are imaged correlates with concepts of women's empowerment and activism.

The project of this chapter is threefold. First is to demonstrate the thesis that Whiteheadian metaphysics and theology are complementary with feminist thought. Second is to experiment with Whiteheadian thought as an integrative theory. Whiteheadian relational epistemology is put to the test of connecting modes of ecological, human, and God-world relationships. If Whiteheadian thought is useful, especially in responding to womanist and ecofeminist thought, then there is a compelling reason to engage in Whiteheadian feminist theology and philosophy. Finally, the remainder of the chapter selects critique of divine omnipotence and construction of relational concepts of power as critical for Whiteheadian feminist metaphysics.

WHITEHEAD ON DIVINE POWER

As a Whiteheadian feminist, I find that process philosophy corroborates my sense of the inadequacy of the classical understanding of divine omnipotence and facilitates my search for a more adequate concept of divine omnipotence. Process philosophers and theologians have articulated a critique of the attribute of omnipotence in classical theism, which reflects sensibilities similar to those of women.

Whitehead (whose philosophy has been shown in previous chapters to be compatible in several respects with feminist thought) is fundamentally critical of divine omnipotence. Whitehead's horror at the traditional concept of God is rooted in the fact that the history of religious thought promotes the association of God with tyrannical power. This sentiment is expressed in *Modes of Thought* in which Whitehead writes,

> When the religious thought of the ancient world from Mesopotamia to Palestine, and from Palestine to Egypt, required terms to express that ultimate unity of direction in the universe, upon which all order depends, and which gives its meaning to importance, they could find no way better to express themselves than by borrowing the characteristics of the touchy, vain, imperious tyrants who ruled the empires of the World. In the origin of civilized religion, Gods are like Dictators. Our modern rituals still retain this taint. The most emphatic repudiations of this archaic notion are to be found scattered in the doctrines of Buddhism and in the Christian Gospels.[28]

With rare exceptions, civilized religions have chosen the image of God as tyrant or dictator to express a sense of God's power and control in the universe. As Whitehead's commentary indicates, this metaphor was a man-made choice from the realm of human experience. Note of course that Whitehead's description of this choice is inflammatory and biased, but this critical reflection on the dictator metaphor compensates for a predominant refusal to criticize this image.

An earlier point, from *Process and Reality*, expresses Whitehead's explicit rejection of the idea of God as ruling Caesar, ruthless moralist, and unmoved mover. The importance of this passage is that it acknowledges within the midst of religious tradition a specific repudiation of the image of God as all-controlling power.

There is, however, in the Galilean origin of Christianity yet another suggestion which does not fit very well with any of the three main strands of thought. It does not emphasize the ruling Caesar, or the ruthless moralist, or the unmoved mover. It dwells upon the tender elements in the world, which slowly and in quietness operate by love; and it finds purpose in the present immediacy of a kingdom not of this world. Love neither rules, nor is it unmoved; also it is a little oblivious as to morals. It does not look to the future; for it finds its own reward in the immediate present.[29]

The contrast between the Galilean vision and the predominant view of God underscores the absurdity of the fact that in the midst of a larger tradition that understood God's power to be like that of the ruling Caesar, there was a countermetaphor. This countermetaphor that places God's omnipotence in the context of power which operates by love has been a suppressed element even in the Christian paradigm community, which professes to hold Christ as a special revelation of God. The fact that this is a choice that creates a logical inconsistency within the Christian tradition suggests perhaps that it has been more important to uphold a particular concept of power than to support the defining paradigm exemplified in Christ.

Cobb on Persuasive Power

John B. Cobb Jr. has compared classical formulations of divine omnipotence with the alternative view of power articulated especially by Charles Hartshorne. In *God and the World*, Cobb refers to the illustrative story of the potter and the potter's clay, which reflects a particular understanding of power. The relationship of the potter and the clay reflects a power relationship that assumes that power is wielded over that which has the incapacity to resist. In this sense of power, the potter has a great deal of power over the clay. As Cobb points out, the nature and quantity of the clay are the only limitations upon the potter's power. Although God's power is similar to the power of the potter, God is omnipotent in that even these limitations do not apply to divine power. Omnipotence suggests that there is one center of power, which is God. Creatures are powerless. The immense power of God is measured against the impotence of the world. Cobb's argument is that this understanding of divine power leads us to question the moral character of God (because God must be fully responsible for sin) and that, in fact, it attributes very little power to God, because there is no competing power.

As an alternative, Cobb explores a conception of power that is placed in the context of multiple centers of power. It is a concept of power in contrast to a divine monopoly on power. Cobb asks us to consider that the only real power is power that influences the power of others. Cobb's example is compelling:

The power too often attributed to God is the power to compel or to force. But in my relations with other people, such as my children, the use of such power is a last resort which expresses my total powerlessness in all ways that matter.[30]

The divine monopoly on power is the power to compel or to force. It is coercive power. However, human experience suggests that coercive power is a power that concedes powerlessness. Unfortunately this pseudopower is the form of power that has been attributed to God. Cobb's assessment of this identification of divine power with coercion is that "it is indeed a wretched and pitiful form of power, and it is astonishing and shocking that this most inferior of all forms of human power should ever have been a model for thinking of divine power."[31]

An alternative form of power is persuasive power. Although coercion is power directed toward others in proportion to their powerlessness, persuasion is power exercised in relation to the powerful. Persuasive power is not efficacious by appeal to self-interest alone. Persuasion depends on relations of respect, concern, and love. It is a form of power that addresses the power and freedom of the other, not to diminish adversarily that power and freedom but to maximize the power and, therefore, the freedom of the other. When this alternative understanding of power is attributed to God, divine "omnipotence" is transformed to mean that God exercises an optimum of power in relation to other centers of power. God urges creatures toward the good rather than coercing adherence to the divine will. This lure toward the good is balanced with the wish to enhance the power/freedom of those whom God seeks to persuade.[32]

Hartshorne on Omnipotence

Charles Hartshorne, in particular, has discussed a conception of divine power more philosophically along with a critique of the classical understanding of divine omnipotence. (This is a pervasive dimension of Hartshorne's thought, which is recently summarized in his book *Omnipotence and Other Theological Mistakes*.) The "mistaken" meaning of omnipotence entails the view that divine power must be the highest conceivable form of power. Take, for example, Richard Swinburne's understanding of divine omnipotence as an interpretation of this highest conceivable form of power: "If God is omnipotent, then he must be able to control by basic actions all states of affairs everywhere."[33] Attaching this classical definition of perfection to God has entailed the conclusion that if God is perfect in power, then God causes and determines all events that occur. The most obvious inconsistencies arise when this view of omnipotence must be reconciled with natural catastrophes and human moral evil. Hartshorne suggests that the views that God either "permits" human sin or that God decides that creatures will perform divinely chosen acts "freely" are theological skirtings of the issue. Such views cannot explain the evils not attributable to human sinfulness nor do they accommodate the presence of chance/risk involved in genuine freedom. Divine goodness, justice, and morality; human freedom and sinfulness; and natural evil remain as major ambiguities and contradictions to be explained by this idea of divine omnipotence. Hartshorne believes that omnipotence under the definition of classical theism entails divine limitation.

> All I have said is that omnipotence as usually conceived is a false or indeed absurd ideal, which in truth *limits* God, denies to him any world worth talking about: a world of living, that is to say, significantly decision-making, agents. It is the *tradition* which did indeed terribly limit divine power, the power to foster creativity even in the least of the creatures.
>
> No worse falsehood was ever perpetrated than the traditional concept of omnipotence. It is a piece of unconscious blasphemy, condemning God to a dead world, probably not distinguishable from no world at all.[34]

Hartshorne's proposal is that some of the ambiguities in the classical conception of God may be resolved by application of the principle of dual transcendence, which says that the description of something as *p* and *not-p* is contradictory only if the predicate and its negation are applied in the same respect to the something that is being described.[35] Consequently, one could understand that divine perfection is absolute perfection in some respects and relative perfection in all others. The neoclassical conception of perfection entails the idea that God is surpassable by no other entity except godself and that God changes. Thus, for example, God loves perfectly all creatures, but God's love is surpassed when God takes in the future joys and sorrows of the world as they increase the divine enrichment. In Hartshorne's language, God may be described as the self-surpassing surpasser.

If the principle of dual transcendence is applied specifically to the question of divine omnipotence, then there may be a mediation between the assertion of and the denial of an all-controlling, deterministic, monopolistic omnipotence. Hartshorne affirms that there is a supreme power that creates and controls the world but that the creatures are centers of decision and power with some capacity for self-determination. Human freedom is rendered meaningful by this mediation through the inclusion of chance, spontaneity, creativity, and decision. The concept of God's power is tempered with the loving appreciation of a deity who influences creatures and cherishes their contributions to the enrichment of divine being.

LOOMER ON RELATIONAL POWER

Bernard Loomer, a process theologian, has described and contrasted two conceptions of power, unilateral power and relational power. Because our descriptions of God are rooted in metaphors and concepts that have their origin in human experience, it is appropriate to reflect further on the conceptions of power in human experience. Feminists may feel an affinity with Loomer due to their mutual dissatisfaction with existing patterns of human relating. Fundamentally, the distortion of human relationships is the product of inadequate concepts of power and selfhood. In a broad sense, this truncated version of relatedness diminishes ecological, socioeconomic, crosscultural, and sexual (or gender-related) interrelationships.

Loomer's term for the distorted/distorting form of power is unilateral or linear power. Characterized as masculine or active in form, unilateral power is concerned to maximize effects upon another, while minimizing reciprocal influences upon oneself. In Loomer's words:

> I define the traditional notion of power as your ability either as a person or a group to shape your environment (regardless of whether the environment consists of things or people) in such a fashion that you can realize your goals. This kind of power has to do with your ability to manipulate, control, utilize, recreate, transform the other—whatever the other is—in such a fashion that you can accomplish your aims. You can determine how much power you have by the size of the environment one can control or by the size of the other that it takes to cause you to change your course of action.
>
> In this kind of power the other exists basically as an instrument for our ends. You are not concerned primarily with the influence of the other upon you. It is masculine whether it is utilized by a man or a woman. This is the traditional conception of power. I call it a military, economic, political, or masculine conception of power.[36]

The effect of unilateral power may be advanced directly or indirectly, persuasively or coercively, but it is always one-sided, abstract, and nonrelational. Unilateral power is nonrelational in the sense that it requires a nonmutual relatedness such that relationships are internal for the powerless and external for the powerful. Such is the power that has controlled Western historical experience, including male/female relationships. Correlative to Loomer's observation that this type of power has allowed men to dominate women and nature is feminist outrage at the consequent pyramid of domination, which allows a minority at the apex of the pyramid to exercise power downward upon powerless people and creatures at the bottom of the hierarchy.

The myth of individualism is the distorted view of selfhood associated with unilateral power. Selfhood is identified with the self-made, self-sufficient, self-dependent individual. The noncommunal, nonsocial self is not constituted by relations with others. The individual seeks to magnify his or her self-sufficiency by utilizing society as an instrument for self-fulfillment. Nonsocial individualism leads to the view that freedom is inherent in the individual and that love is essentially one way of effecting or exercising power over others. As a singular self, the individual loves out of concern and responsibility for the other and not out of personal need for love or the capacity to respond to the other. Thus, unilateral love and unilateral power go hand in hand and the ideals of self-sufficiency and independence become so highly glorified that they are deified.

Loomer's evaluation of relationships based on unilateral power focuses on consequent "life-denying injustices."[37] Within this conception of power, self-worth is a matter of competition and superior status. Personal power means claiming dominance in the context of inequality. The instrument for self-fulfillment is the other whose influences and freedom are intentionally curtailed that one's own freedom and power may be maximized. The strong become pretentious about their self-importance. Their claims and strengths are overplayed, and their weaknesses are ignored. Inequalities become the locus of estrangement between the weak and the strong until finally both the strong and the weak are impoverished and natural inequalities based on difference generate injustice.

As victims of injustice, women have sought hope in a vision of reality that promotes interdependence, relationality, and connectedness. The web is a metaphor that depicts interconnectedness for both feminists and Bernard Loomer. As Loomer imaged the web, he said:

> As I define it, the web is the world conceived of as an indefinitely extended complex of interrelated, interdependent events or units of reality. This includes the human and nonhuman, the organic and inorganic levels of life and existence.[38]

Loomer also wrote that

> We start with the notion of the Web as a world in which the entities in it, including the people, are bound together as inter-related. We are dependent upon each other, and yet each claims a kind of independence from all that goes on. The higher one goes in the evolutionary scale, the greater the concern for independence, but one never loses the sense of dependence upon the others within the context of an environment in which one lives and moves and has his or her being.[39]

From this depiction of the interdependence of the world, Loomer envisioned an alternative conception of power and selfhood.

Loomer's alternative to unilateral power is not a feminine or passive form of power. In other words, it does not involve the capacity only to receive an influence from another, because this would simply reverse the valuation of the poles of inequality. Relational power "is the capacity both to influence others and to be influenced by others."[40] It is a matter both of giving and receiving. Loomer was concerned to show that relational power is a more humanizing form of power, which promotes human fulfillment. This conception promotes mutuality and operates under the assumption that the capacity to incorporate the influence of another is as powerful as the ability to influence.

Relational power means that relationships involve mutual internal relatedness, such that all members of the relationship are constituted by their interdependence. As Loomer describes it:

> Power is the capacity to sustain a mutually internal relationship. This is a relationship of mutually influencing and being influenced, of mutually giving and receiving, of mutually making claims and permitting and enabling others to make their claims. This is a relation of mutuality which embraces all the dimensions and kinds of inequality that the human spirit is heir to. The principle of equality most profoundly means that we are equally dependent on the constitutive relationships that create us, however relatively unequal we are in our various strengths, including our ability to exemplify the fullness and concreteness of this kind of power.[41]

Mutual internal relatedness provides a basis for equality even though the individuals in the relationship are unequal in their strengths and capacities.

As a corollary to relational power, the individual is not self-dependent and self-sufficient, but communal. The individual is self-creating yet constituted by the society. The individual lives in the society, and the society lives in the individual. As self-creating, the individual chooses to receive influences from others. Thus, the individual is constituted by the influences of the society. The other becomes part of one's being, part of the fabric of one's life. Then, reciprocally, the individual contributes his or her influences on other individuals in the society. Freedom arises in the connectedness of the web both as the emergence of self-creativity in the individual and as the gift of the constitutive relations of the society.

Loomer believed that relational power aims at enhancing those relationships that include individuals and groups of stature and size. Refer again to Loomer's definition of size, the capacity to integrate diverse relationships into the fabric of oneself without losing or threatening the integrity of selfhood and the correlative concern to enable others to increase in stature.[42] Size is a somewhat deceptive concept, because it could easily be confused with a proliferation of superficial external relationships. Instead, size must be interpreted within the context of mutual internal relatedness, relational power, and freedom born of connectedness. Size is an idea that suggests that inequalities and diversity may be transformative of selfhood, that self-creation is enhanced by the influences of the community, and that selfhood is, in fact, diminished apart from community.

BROCK ON EROTIC POWER

Rita Nakashima Brock, Japanese–Puerto Rican and Whiteheadian feminist, appreciatively applies Loomer's analysis of the two conceptions of power to her fundamental thesis that men and women operate with different understandings of power. What Loomer referred to as unilateral power, Brock characterizes as the power that delivers death. This is a patriarchal form of power. A dualistic, oppositional, hierarchical worldview of patriarchy supports a conception of power that is competitive and nonrelational. This power is ego-centered, because it is based upon the priority of individuation and autonomy. It assumes a "fixed sum" understanding of power such that one person's power gain necessitates another's power loss. A patriarchal value hierarchy is based on quantification of power. Consequently, patriarchal power is a concept that justifies oppression, including and not limited to oppression of women.

A feminist view of self and power is not merely an alternative but a critique of patriarchal power, and it makes the claim of greater inclusivity. Brock names this power "erotic power." Erotic power supports both self-identity and relational connections. Erotic power connects us with our multidimensioned (physical, spiritual, intellectual, emotional, sensual) selves and extends that connection, affirmation, and identification to others. This power sees the strengths in interdependence and giving. Brock characterizes this power as the power that nurtures life. In contrast to a "fixed sum" theory of power, erotic power is based on generosity and the conviction that one's self-realization is dependent on contributing to the self-realization of others.

Brock is no exception to feminist theologians who follow the method of beginning with women's experience as the basis of theology. Women's experience of oppressive forms of power and of their own sense of a relational form of power is a major resource for formulation of an understanding of God. Women's experience of power provides both a critique of the classical understanding of divine omnipotence, as well as the suggestion of a new vision of God's power.

Brock joins the feminist claim that God is imaged as male and, in particular, that God's power is a masculine form of power. For patriarchy, if God possesses the highest conceivable form of power, then God possesses patriarchal power. This is apparently as high as patriarchal conceptions can reach. Patriarchal omnipotence is a projection of masculine power mythology, which infuses even the benevolent metaphors for God. Even God's love, *agape*, is a unilateral power, which makes creatures powerless even in their imitative love for each other and God. Because this oppressive form of power is attributed to God, God becomes the justification for the perpetuation of oppression. Patriarchal institutions (whether abstract or concrete) are resistant to modification of divine omnipotence in favor of alternative conceptions of power, because their systems are grounded in a patriarchal form of power.

It is no accident Christian theology has been reluctant to give ground in the use of a male image system. Theology has tied itself to patriarchal power and a masculine view of reality. Although other, less patriarchal views have survived within Christianity, theological systems and ecclesiastical institutions with hierarchical understandings of power have been the most reluctant to disconnect themselves from their identification with patriarchal power and its built-in misogyny.[43]

I would add that it becomes irrelevant to debate the logical consistency of classical theism if it continues to support oppression and misogyny. There are times when it becomes necessary to reject even the most consistent perceptions of reality.

If we reject classical theism and its understanding of divine omnipotence, Brock proposes a theology of erotic power to be adopted in its stead. A theology of erotic power is centered in the view that all things are interconnected (all things participate in mutual internal relations). In this perspective, God's omnipotence is erotic power. God's power is understood in relation to God's love. God's erotic omnipotence then provides a paradigm for just relationships in the world. As Brock describes this omnipotence and its influences on human relatedness, she writes:

> The world exists as evidence of a loving divine spirit, and that spirit is present to us in our connectedness to and our concern and care for ourselves and others. Divine reality does not consist of a will outwardly imposed upon the world from a transcendent deity, but in our awareness of the very nature of erotic power as that which emerges from within our deepest connection to ourselves, and from our experience of God in the life-giving, creative power of interdependence. God as loving is present to us through our relationships to self and others. Divine will is not found in the imposition of external, abstract goals and principles upon a reluctant humanity.[44]

Erotic power is foundational for Brock's proposal of the metaphor God as Heart. Brock deemphasizes the sentimental connotations of heart in favor of its holistic imagery. Heart depicts the wholeness, vitality, and centeredness of human selfhood, including the union of the body, spirit, reason, and passion.[45] Heart also carries a holistic relational perspective. In addition to the intimacy of the self and its various aspects, Heart suggests the intimacy and connection of self and others. The Heart seeks out connections.[46] As a metaphor for God, particularly through Christ, Heart is the incarnation of erotic power. Erotic power is revealed in human existence as a revelation of human "existence in relationship and our cocreation of each other."[47] "[D]ivine erotic power is the Heart of the Universe."[48]

Using Brock's insights in summary fashion, there are three major points to be emphasized in a feminist critique of the classical understanding of divine omnipotence. First, a masculine interpretation of divine power is based on the presupposition that the power of God, the highest conceivable form of power, is patriarchal power. Second, patriarchal power is not the only form of power in human experience. Women's experience and exercise of power suggest an alternate interpretation of the meaning of power. Third, masculine, unilateral, despotic power is inadequate as a metaphor for divine omnipotence, essentially on the grounds that it is misogynist. It is a power metaphor that creates an oppressive image of God unworthy of worship, because it is not reflective of women's experience and it is idolatrous of patriarchal conceptions of power. Brock offers erotic power as a form of power more inclusive of women's experience of power and proposes the image of God as Heart as a liberating metaphor.

GOD IN WHITEHEADIAN FEMINIST PERSPECTIVE

One of the challenging issues facing theology today is the problem of oppression. If theology is to make Christian faith meaningful to the contemporary world, it must address the fact that people, nature, and the earth itself suffer injustice. Christian faith must be a liberating faith.

My particular experience fits into the larger category of women's experience, a part of which includes the experiences of the oppression of women as women in relation to their other social identities. One of the issues that concerns me is how (and indeed whether) Christian faith can be liberating for women. On this point, evidence from women's experience, from my personal experience, is ambivalent. On one hand, many women witness to the liberation and hope that faith in Christ has brought to their lives. On the other hand, both Christian and postchristian women cast a critical eye toward Christianity as a source of women's oppression.

How shall we respond to the criticism that patriarchal Christian images and concepts are irrelevant to women's experience and idolatrous of male experience?[49] My response is that this is, in fact, generally true of both the biblical tradition and the church, but that we are not without liberating images for women in Christian scripture and history. By focusing on these liberating metaphors and creating new images, theology especially offers a liberating interpretation of Christian faith for women.

One of the most important connections between process theology and women's experience is that both are concerned with rethinking the meaning of power. Women have experienced oppression in the context of hierarchical power, which is institutionalized in society and theology. One feminist project is to imagine and experience new meanings of power in human relationships. Process theology is equally critical of hierarchical forms of power. Consequently, a most significant contribution of process theology is a reconstruction of the concept of God and divine omnipotence. It is my perspective that process theology has a liberating alternative theism to offer feminist constructive theology. This chapter is an exposition of my Whiteheadian feminist perspective, which answers two questions: What is the alternative theism of process theology? How is it reflective of women's experience and liberating for some women?

A central feature of process theology is dipolar theism, which means that God's existence may be described as having two inseparable poles or aspects, much like two dimensions of a human personality that characterize the individual without fragmenting her personal integrity. The first aspect of God's dipolarity is called the primordial nature of God.

The primordial nature of God is the eternal pole of God's existence, which could be described as the realm of divine creative imagination. In the primordial nature, God envisions ideals, which the philosopher Whitehead called eternal objects. These ideals are pure possibilities such as goodness, truth, or beauty and geometrical forms or mathematics. Pure possibilities are abstractions, which God must make relevant for the world. Taking account of actual persons, events, and situations, God imagines how goodness, for example, could be actualized in particular events. In other words, God imagines how pure, abstract possibilities could be real possibilities for individuals in their concrete circumstances. In my case, taking account of my history, books I have read, my education, my religious experience and commitments, important personal relationships, physical health and abilities, and intellect (all of which God knows well), God might best imagine real possibilities for me, which embody or incarnate goodness, truth, and beauty—most likely a career involving theological reflection rather than professional basketball given my actual aptitudes and background. The real possibilities are envisioned by uniquely interweaving my particular life and the eternal objects to create concrete potentials for me. It is God's creative act in my life that I feel and respond to what God has imagined for me. I may experience these real possibilities for my life as an unconscious longing for novelty, an unspeakable attraction to a future option, an irresistible appetite for life. Whitehead called this experience "the lure of God." John Cobb refers to it as "the call forward."[50] It is not unlike what Christian faith has described as the call of God in our lives.

The primordial nature of God is responsible for God's creative activity in the world. To describe God's primordial nature is to speak of God as Creator in a sense unique to process theology. John Cobb and David Griffin have said that the primordial nature is expressive of God as "creative love."[51] My way of understanding what this means is to compare creative love with the love of a mother for her children.[52] A good mother knows her children well. She remembers when they began to walk, she knows how well they have performed in school, she watches them at play, she listens to their dreams, she hears their crying, she feels their affection, she hopes that their futures are bright and happy. A mother loves her children for who they are and what they may become, in their actuality and potentiality. Good mothers encourage their children to realize their best possibilities. This is true of the mother's love for each of her children. Mother love avoids favoritism, because it cherishes the uniqueness of each child. Mother love is a lure for her children's unique potentials. A mother is touched profoundly by the uniqueness of each child, and her love and nurture reflect this experience. It is the same with God's creative love, which recognizes our individuality and encourages us to attain our best possibilities.

What does the power of God mean in light of God's creative love? First of all, God's power is not coercive, irresistible, controlling power over others but the alternative of persuasive or relational power. If we return to our example of the good mother, we imagine that ideally this mother avoids using coercive power to compel her children to study, practice, and succeed. To coerce her children would diminish their self-esteem, motivation, and growth by rendering them powerless and curtailing their freedom. The exercise of coercive power would amount to the mother's admission that she had lost control, that she had broken the rapport established in her relationship with her children, that she had failed with reasoning and encouragement, that she was reduced to the exercise of force. Coercive power leaves the powerful and the powerless feeling diminished, helpless, and dehumanized. Under better circumstances, the good mother seeks to persuade her children. Through discussion, participation, guidance, and motivation, the good mother influences her children. Respecting the particular interests and concerns of the children, the mother contributes a favorable environment and enticement for the flowering of her children's abilities. The children learn to use their freedom wisely. They experience a sense of their own creativity and self-motivation. The children are empowered.

The creative love of God is really more like *eros*, understood correctly, than *agape*, and the relational, persuasive power of God may well be called erotic power. Sam Keen describes the original meaning of *eros* in contrast to a distorted meaning that limits *eros* to sexual interpretation. Plato's myth of the androgyne depicts erotic love and desire as a longing to be reunited with our missing complement.[53] In Greek philosophy, *eros* was considered love that functioned as prime mover, the motivating principle for human and nonhuman alike, an impulse that creates yearning and striving for fulfillment, indwelling promise, and potentiality. *Eros* is a power that moves and propels life from potentiality to actuality.[54] *Eros* is an ontological love that informs who we are and links us to the web of life.[55] It is appropriate that Whitehead linked Plato's *eros* to the primordial nature of God. *Eros* as the urge toward realization of perfection fits the creative nature of Whitehead's God. The primordial nature of God as a lure toward novelty and possibility is the *eros* that beckons the creation of a new event from a synthesis of the past.[56] Brock's concept of erotic power arises out of the original meaning of *eros* and Whitehead's view of God as *Eros*. The image of mother love is enhanced by associating the divine mother love with *eros*, because it captures the sense that the love of the mother and othermothers is creative for the child and the mother herself and that the creativity of motherself is a lure for the child's potential.

Returning to the dipolar nature of God, we now consider the consequent nature of God. The consequent nature completes an image of God's relationship with the world and with individual creatures. Creatures who respond to the creative love of God remain free to choose how they will act. They may accept or refuse God's persuasive lure. To this extent, creatures determine who they become. Once the creature has actualized his or her choice, the interaction between God and the creature has not ended, because God finally responds to the creature's choice. God's response is a feeling of the experience of the creature. God empathizes with the creature's experience—rejoicing with the creature whose experience is rich and suffering with the creature who suffers. God feels this experience as if it were God's own experience. With this immediate feeling, the experience becomes God's experience and everlastingly resides in God's consequent nature.

Because of the consequent nature of God, there is mutuality between the creature and the Creator in the sense that God contributes to the formation of each creature by the divine lure, and each creature contributes to the being of God by adding new experience to the consequent nature. For process theologians, this mutuality between God and the creature is a special instance of the doctrine of internal relations, which says that each creature is constituted by its relationships. This is true of God (whom Whitehead calls a creature) and the creatures. Our experiences are our relationships. Who I am is not merely a matter of statistics about my height, weight, and coloring. My identity is formed significantly by relationships with friends, family, colleagues, nature, and God. The same is true of God whose identity is formed significantly by relationships with people, nonhuman animals, vegetables, and inorganic nature.

The love of God in the consequent nature is responsive love.[57] It is love that appreciates, evaluates, and incorporates the creature. We may borrow an image from Hebrew scripture that emerges from an exegesis of the word *rachamim*, which is usually translated compassion. *Rachamim* could more appropriately be translated "womb-love," because it shares a common triliteral root with the word "womb" (*rechem*). God's compassion or *rachamim* is nurturing love, tenderness, and the security of the mother's womb. It suggests the kind of identification of mother with child that creates bonding and intensification of love. Although it is an imperfect metaphor for the consequent nature of God, the love of a mother for her unborn child resembles the responsive love of God. Imagine the experience of a woman in her last month of pregnancy. The unborn child is certainly nothing to be ignored in her experience. The mother responds to the needs of her child, and the experiences of the child are, in fact, the mother's experiences. For months, the child's hunger determines the mother's nutritional needs and cravings. The mother's body prepares to produce milk. Physical distress on the part of the child becomes physical distress for the mother. The mother feels the child's wakefulness. The movement of the child kicking and punching at its surroundings is movement in the mother's body. This intimacy results in the bonding of mother and child. The mother's love is evident even before the birth of the child. Her responsive love is apparent in her preparation for the child's birth. Prenatal medical care, diet, exercise, shopping, and knitting express the mother's love for the child who is part of her. The baby is clearly an independent individual, but it is also an interdependent part of the mother. The mother's loving relationship with her baby is like that of God who responds to the independent creature and includes the creature in the divine consequent nature.

What I have just described as the dipolar character of God, the dynamic relationship of the primordial and consequent natures of God, is a fruitful conceptual and metaphorical influence on some ecofeminism. The intimate connection between the creative and responsive love of God is panentheistic. Sallie McFague interprets Whiteheadian dipolar theism as an organic model, metaphorically describing the world as God's body, and she integrates the organic model with an agential model, picturing God as the spirit of the body.[58] McFague chooses to refer to Spirit, rather than Mind of God, meaning by Spirit "Breath" or source of life and vitality. Spirit or Breath depicts God's interaction with the world as a relationship rather than control of the order and direction of nature.[59] McFague's panentheism imagines God's creative action as empowerment. "Within this model of the universe as God's body, God's presence and action are evident as the breath of life that gives all bodies, all forms of matter, the energy or power to become themselves."[60] The world as God's body symbolizes both unity and diversity in the world and represents the locus of God's liberating, healing, and inclusive love.[61] Consequently, justice means activism on behalf of bodies, both ecological and human, to see that basic needs for food, shelter, and well-being are met.[62] Rosemary Ruether, similarly influenced by process theism, suggests that Christian tradition is large enough to encompass two voices of divinity, Gaia and God. Ruether's ecological, feminist interpretation of Gaia incorporates much of Whiteheadian dipolar theism or panentheism.

> Compassion for all living things fills our spirits, breaking down the illusion of otherness. At this moment we can encounter the matrix of energy of the universe that sustains the dissolution and recomposition of matter as also a heart that knows us even as we are known. Is there also a consciousness that remembers and envisions and reconciles all things, as the Process theologians believe? Surely, if we are kin to all things and offspring of the universe, then what has flowered in us as consciousness must also be reflected in that universe as well, in the ongoing creative Matrix of the whole.

> As we gaze into the void of our future extinguished self and dissolving substance, we encounter there the wellspring of life and creativity from which all things have sprung and into which they return, only to well up again in new forms. But we also know this as the great Thou, the personal center of the universal process, with which all the small centers of personal being dialogue in the conversation that continually creates and recreates the world. The small selves and the Great Self are finally one, for as She bodies forth in us, all the beings respond in the bodying forth of their diverse creative work that makes the world.[63]

Ruether's description of Gaia reflects the poetry of dipolar theism, even accessing the metaphor of the divine body, which appears prior to Ruether's and McFague's use in Charles Hartshorne's process theism.[64]

God, who is intimately related to the world, is the primary exemplar of one who has the capacity to influence and to be influenced. The primordial nature and the consequent nature characterize God as a being who influences creatures and responds to creaturely influences. Perhaps we may make a bold step in defining divine omnipotence by saying that the power of God is manifest in both God's effect on the world and the world's effect on God. In being the one who creates and the one who is created, God is powerful.

How might redefining "omnipotence" as persuasive power or relational power be liberating to women? First, we must acknowledge that the way we envision God's power shapes the way we exercise power over others. If God's power is coercive, then the highest conceivable form of power is coercive, and humans will emulate that exercise of power. If divine power is power over the powerless, then we will reduce others to powerlessness in order to wield power. If divine power is unilateral or hierarchical or masculine or patriarchal, then we may feel justified or righteous in imitating that ideal form of power. The kind of power that I have just described has been attributed to God. In the hands of its human imitators, it has become the power that oppresses.

We have entertained the idea that persuasive power and relational power may be preferable concepts of power, which do justice to the meaning of omnipotence. The philosopher Whitehead suggested the oddity of describing God as all-controlling power in contrast to the tenderness of the power of Christ. What Whitehead sees is the absurdity of our image of God's power. Christians claim that the revelation of God in Jesus, the Galilean, is central to faith, yet have chosen to compare God with a ruling Caesar. Whitehead reminds Christians to remember Jesus. If Jesus is truly the revelation of God, then God's power cannot be coercive. It must be tender and it must operate by love. Applying the Galilean criterion to persuasive power and relational power, we find that they are a better description of divine power.

Persuasive power and relational power are also more just. Imitating God's power as persuasive and relational is a step toward liberating and empowering those oppressed by intersecting systems of sexism, racism, classism, heterosexism, and speciesism. First, we no longer understand that power involves the separation of people into the powerful and the powerless, the oppressors and the oppressed. Empowering oppressed women does not diminish the power of the oppressors. Oppressive males need not fear that they will be rendered powerless if women also have power. Second, we no longer think of power as power exercised over others in a controlling manner. This mitigates the pyramid of domination, which concentrates power in a small apex of the privileged who have power over women, so-called minorities, and nature. Power is not control; it is the capacity to affect others and to be affected by others. Third, power becomes a relational concept. Freedom and power have their only genuine meanings in the context of relationships, but it is unnecessary to focus on a competitive view of power in relationships. We may think of ourselves as interdependent. What enhances my power and freedom may very well enhance your own. Women will be liberated in male-female relationships when both men and women concentrate on their mutuality. Mutual respect, concern, and love are the proper environment for expressing power and empowerment. Finally, we may remember in our relationships that God's power is liberating. God envisions that each man and woman is a creature with unique potential, and God's aim is that each person may actualize his or her potential. God is not preferential in love for men or women, for one ethnic community over another, for humans or nature—we are valued, not stereotyped, by God in both creative and responsive love. In God's justice and judgment that suffers with the oppressed, we are all liberated by God's divine lure toward full humanity. God promotes rich experience, the creative result of mutual relationships.

NOTES

1. Mary Daly, *Beyond God the Father: Toward a Philosophy of Women's Liberation* (Boston: Beacon Press, 1973), 19.
2. Ibid., 9, 34.
3. Letty M. Russell, *The Future of Partnership* (Philadelphia: Westminster Press, 1979), 33.
4. Rosemary Radford Ruether, *Sexism and God-Talk: Toward a Feminist Theology* (Boston: Beacon Press, 1983), 69.
5. Ibid., 71.
6. Delores S. Williams, *Sisters in the Wilderness: The Challenge of Womanist God-Talk* (Maryknoll, N.Y.: Orbis Books, 1993), 194.
7. Ibid., 196.
8. Ibid., 144, 147.
9. Ibid., 198.
10. Ibid.
11. Ibid., 196.
12. Chung Hyun Kyung, *Struggle to Be the Sun Again: Introducing Asian Women's Theology* (Maryknoll, N.Y.: Orbis Books, 1993), 39.
13. Ibid., 47.
14. Ibid., 50.
15. Ibid., 51.
16. Starhawk, *Dreaming the Dark: Magic, Sex & Politics* (Boston: Beacon Press, 1982), 9.
17. Alice Walker, *The Color Purple* (New York: Washington Square Press, 1982), 178.
18. Ibid., 179.
19. Ibid.
20. Sallie McFague, *Models of God: Theology for an Ecological, Nuclear Age* (Philadelphia: Fortress Press, 1987), 33.
21. Ibid., 39.
22. Ibid., 65.
23. Ibid., 32.
24. Ibid., 73–74.
25. See chapters 4, 5, and 6 of *Models of God*.
26. Mary Daly, *Gyn/Ecology: The Metaethics of Radical Feminism* (Boston: Beacon Press, 1978), xii.
27. Chung, *The Struggle to Be the Sun Again*, 48–49.
28. Alfred North Whitehead, *Modes of Thought* (New York: Macmillan Company, 1938), 68.
29. Alfred North Whitehead, *Process and Reality: Corrected Edition*, ed. David Ray Griffin and Donald W. Sherburne (New York: Free Press, 1978), 343.
30. John B. Cobb Jr., *God and the World* (Philadelphia: Westminster Press, 1969), 89.
31. Ibid., 90.
32. I make reference to persuasive power duly cautioned by Rita Nakashima Brock's critique of this terminology: "While persuasion suggests mutuality and egalitarianism, it continues to connote the actor who may intentionally affect another's behavior through an effective use of the power she or he possesses." Rita Nakashima Brock, *Journeys by Heart: A Christology of Erotic Power* (New York: Crossroad, 1988), 34.
33. Richard Swinburne, *The Existence of God* (Oxford: Clarendon Press, 1979), 97.

34. Charles Hartshorne, *Omnipotence and Other Theological Mistakes* (Albany: State University of New York Press, 1984), 17–18.

35. Ibid., 45.

36. Bernard Loomer, *Unfoldings: Conversations from the Sunday Morning Seminars of Bernard Loomer* (Berkeley, Calif.: First Unitarian Church of Berkeley, 1985), 47.

37. Bernard Loomer, "Two Conceptions of Power," *Process Studies* 6, no. 1 (Spring 1976): 6.

38. Loomer, *Unfoldings*, 1.

39. Ibid., 21.

40. Loomer, "Two Conceptions of Power," 17.

41. Ibid., 22.

42. Bernard Loomer, "S-I-Z-E," *Criterion* 13 (Spring 1974): 6.

43. Rita Nakashima Brock, "Power, Peace, and the Possibility of Survival," in *God and Global Justice: Religion and Poverty in an Unequal World*, ed. Frederick Ferré and Rita H. Mataragnon (New York: Paragon House; New Era Books, 1985), 29.

44. Ibid., 30.

45. Brock, *Journeys by Heart*, xiv.

46. Ibid., 45.

47. Ibid., 46.

48. Ibid.

49. This charge is made by Christain revisionist and feminist Sallie McFague in *Metaphorical Theology: Models of God in Religious Language* (Philadelphia: Fortress Press, 1982), 145.

50. Cobb, *God and the World*, 45.

51. John B. Cobb Jr., and David Ray Griffin, *Process Theology: An Introductory Exposition* (Philadelphia: Westminster Press, 1969), 48.

52. See chapter 3. I first discuss this interpretation with respect to hierarchy in nature.

53. Sam Keen, *The Passionate Life: Stages of Loving* (San Francisco: Harper & Row, 1983), 4.

54. Ibid., 5.

55. Ibid., 25.

56. Alfred North Whitehead, *Adventures of Ideas* (New York: Free Press, 1967), 275.

57. Cobb and Griffin, *Process Theology*, 43.

58. Sallie McFague, *The Body of God: An Ecological Theology* (Minneapolis: Fortress Press, 1993), 135. My interpretation of Whiteheadian metaphysics differs somewhat from McFague's interpretation. McFague interprets process theism as pantheism and then needs to supplement the model with an agential model, but I interpret the consequent nature of God as the world and the primordial nature as the mental or spiritual pole of deity; hence, I contend that process theism is already panentheistic and entails the characteristics of the agential model that McFague proposes as a supplement.

59. Ibid., 145.

60. Ibid., 148.

61. Ibid., 84, 129.

62. Ibid., 18.

63. Rosemary Radford Ruether, *Gaia and God: An Ecofeminist Theology of Earth Healing* (New York: HarperCollins; HarperSanFrancisco, 1992), 252–53.

64. Charles Hartshorne, *Omnipotence and Other Theological Mistakes*, 54–56.

Beginning a Relationship, Beginning a Cosmology

THE POINT OF THE previous chapters has been to show that a constructive feminist cosmology may be based on the relational philosophy of Alfred North Whitehead. Whitehead's philosophy is particularly appropriate to the task not only because it complements feminist theory, but because it is a conceptual framework that assumes the reality and importance of relatedness. As an open system, Whitehead's philosophy accommodates new constructive efforts to say what those relationships may be. The value of Whiteheadian philosophy for this constructive project should not subordinate or detract from the autonomy of feminist thought. I have proposed that feminists may freely adopt and adapt Whiteheadian thought to evoke feminist ideas, experiences, and expression.

Although feminists do not need to rely on Whitehead, I have attempted to demonstrate that Whitehead's philosophy complements and may enhance feminist thinking. The complementarity of Whiteheadian thought and feminist thought is itself an enhancement of feminist perspectives in that it adds another voice in solidarity with feminist criticisms of the status quo and constructions of postmodern alternatives. In particular, I have relied heavily on Whitehead's doctrine of internal relations as a conceptual tool for reflection on the relationships of humans and nature, women and the human community, and humans and God. Whitehead funds a new perspective on the relationship of humans and nature by evoking a focus on intrinsic value in nature and a high valuation of diversity in creation. The doctrine of internal relations is a Whiteheadian basis for emphasizing the worldliness of feminist separatism and examining the efficacy of separatism and female friendship to change patriarchal, hierarchical, and oppressive systems. The internal relationship of God and the world is an important part of an alternative Whiteheadian theism, which reinterprets power in relationships. Not only is Whitehead's thought a valuable conceptual tool for expressing and integrating feminist concerns, it has the potential to contribute to the empowerment of women in their relatedness.

Aware of significant limitations in my knowledge and experience, my attempt to imagine a feminist cosmology rests as a proposal offered with humility and in anticipation of criticism. First, I am aware that the assumptions and method formative of this proposal do not conform with some mainstream philosophical/theological scholarship. A feminist cosmology concerned with ecological, antihierarchical relationships rather than hierarchy, with diverse and relative contexts rather than universals, with interdisciplinary rather than disciplinary sources and method, and with relational rather than atomistic foci risks academic credibility. Among postmodernists (some of whom are feminists), a feminist cosmology sympathetic to metaphysics and constructive postmodernism as a goad toward activism risks the emptiness of meaninglessness and deconstruction itself. A feminist cosmology is susceptible to criticism from feminists for participation in abstract forms of thought and expression rather than concrete and accessible ideas and for participation in ostensibly, perhaps complicitous, optimistic and reconciling conclusions. A feminist cosmology is most vulnerable to womanist criticism for its intended scope, which is handicapped by the difficulty in realistically interpreting experiences that are not my own, by education that ill-prepared me with information about history and cultures not my own, and by any universalizing tendencies bound to philosophical systems, however committed to dynamic relational contexts.

Cautioned by the difficulties attending construction of a feminist cosmology, I tentatively continue the project with the understanding that feminist cosmology must be responsive and dialogical. I undertook the project not to arrive deductively at a final and flawless system that I intend to impose on women or communities but to respond tentatively and inductively to ecofeminist, Third World, and womanist claims. Without universalizing or ghettoizing my experience and ideas, my intention has been to find words and ideas that integrate diverse criticisms and alternative perspectives that make a claim on my conscience, integrity, and ethics. To these ends, feminist cosmology must be dialogical and dynamic, willing to change and act responsively, as well as descriptive of contrasts and evocative of creative praxis. My best hope is that the beginning of a feminist cosmology is the beginning of a relationship with those who will criticize, challenge, and inspire growth of a relational, responsive feminist perspective.

BIBLIOGRAPHY

Adair, Margo, and Sharon Howell. "The Subjective Side of Power." In *Healing the Wounds: The Promise of Ecofeminism.* Edited by Judith Plant. Philadelphia: New Society Publishers, 1989.

Armstrong-Buck, Susan. "Nonhuman Experience: A Whiteheadian Analysis." *Process Studies* 18, no. 1 (Spring 1989): 1–18.

The Biology and Gender Study Group. "The Importance of Feminist Critique for Contemporary Cell Biology." In *Feminism and Science.* Edited by Nancy Tuana. Bloomington: Indiana University Press, 1985.

Birch, Charles, and John B. Cobb Jr. *The Liberation of Life: From the Cell to the Community.* Cambridge: Cambridge University Press, 1981.

Brock, Rita Nakashima. *Journeys by Heart: A Christology of Erotic Power.* New York: Crossroad, 1988.

———. "Power, Peace, and the Possibility of Survival." In *God and Global Justice: Religion and Poverty in an Unequal World.* Edited by Frederick Ferré and Rita H. Mataragnon. New York: Paragon House, New Era Books, 1985.

Carson, Rachel. *Silent Spring.* Boston: Houghton Mifflin Company, 1962.

Chodorow, Nancy. *The Reproduction of Mothering: Psychoanalysis and the Sociology of Gender.* Berkeley: University of California Press, 1978.

Chung Hyun Kyung. *Struggle to Be the Sun Again: Introducing Asian Women's Theology.* Maryknoll, N.Y.: Orbis Books, 1990.

Cobb, John B. Jr. *God and the World.* Philadelphia: Westminster Press, 1969.

———. "The Intrapsychic Structure of Christian Existence." *Journal of the American Academy of Religion* 36 (December 1968): 327–39.

———. "Strengthening the Spirit." *Union Seminary Quarterly Review* 30 (Winter-Summer 1975): 130–39.

Cobb, John B. Jr., and David Ray Griffin. *Process Theology: An Introductory Exposition.* Philadelphia: Westminster Press, 1969.

Collins, Patricia Hill. *Black Feminist Thought: Knowledge, Consciousness, and the Politics of Empowerment.* New York: Routledge, 1990.

Daly, Mary. *Beyond God the Father: Toward a Philosophy of Women's Liberation.* Boston: Beacon Press, 1973.

———. *Gyn/Ecology: The Metaethics of Radical Feminism.* Boston: Beacon Press, 1978.

———. *Pure Lust: Elemental Feminist Philosophy.* Boston: Beacon Press, 1978.

Daly, Mary, in cahoots with Jane Caputi. *Websters' First New Intergalactic Wickedary of the English Language.* Boston: Beacon Press, 1987.

Davis, Angela. *Women, Race and Class.* New York: Random House; Vintage Books, 1983.

Doubiago, Sharon. "Mama Coyote Talks to the Boys." In *Healing the Wounds: The Promise of Ecofeminism.* Edited by Judith Plant. Philadelphia: New Society Publishers, 1989.

Douglas, Kelly Brown. *The Black Christ.* Maryknoll, N.Y.: Orbis Books, 1994.

Eugene, Toinette M. "On 'Difference' and the Dream of Pluralistic Feminism." *Journal of Feminist Studies in Religion* 8, no. 2 (Fall 1992): 91–98.

Farley, Margaret A. *Personal Commitments: Beginning, Keeping, Changing*. San Francisco: Harper & Row, 1986.

Gearhart, Sally Miller. *The Wanderground: Stories of the Hill Women*. Boston: Alyson Publications, 1979.

Gilligan, Carol. *In a Different Voice: Psychological Theory and Women's Development*. Cambridge: Harvard University Press, 1982.

Grant, Jacquelyn. *White Women's Christ and Black Women's Jesus: Feminist Christology and Womanist Response*. Atlanta, Ga.: Scholars Press, 1989.

Griffin, Susan. "Split Culture." In *Healing the Wounds: The Promise of Ecofeminism*. Edited by Judith Plant. Philadelphia: New Society Publishers, 1989.

———. *Woman and Nature: The Roaring Inside Her*. New York: Harper & Row; Colophon Books, 1978.

Haraway, Donna. *Primate Visions: Gender, Race, and Nature in the World of Modern Science*. New York: Routledge, 1989.

Harrison, Beverly Wildung. *Our Right to Choose: Toward a New Ethic of Abortion*. Boston: Beacon Press, 1983.

Hartshorne, Charles. *Omnipotence and Other Theological Mistakes*. Albany: State University of New York Press, 1984.

Hill, William J. "Two Gods of Love: Aquinas and Whitehead." *Listening* 14, no. 3 (Fall 1979): 258–59.

hooks, bell. *Feminist Theory: From Margin to Center*. Boston: South End Press, 1984.

Howell, Nancy R. "The Promise of a Process Feminist Theory of Relations." *Process Studies* 17, no. 2 (Summer 1988): 78–87.

———. "Radical Relatedness and Feminist Separatism." *Process Studies* 18, no. 2 (Summer 1989): 118–26.

Hunt, Mary E. *Fierce Tenderness: A Feminist Theology of Friendship*. New York: Crossroad, 1991.

Hurston, Zora Neale. *Their Eyes Were Watching God*. Urbana and Chicago: University of Illinois Press, 1978.

Isasi-Díaz, Ada María. "Viva la Diferencia!" *Journal of Feminist Studies in Religion* 8, no. 2 (Fall 1992): 98–102.

Isasi-Díaz, Ada María, and Yolanda Tarango. *Hispanic Women: Prophetic Voice in the Church*. Minneapolis: Fortress Press, 1992.

Jordan, Judith V. "The Meaning of Mutuality." In *Women's Growth in Connection: Writings from the Stone Center*, by Judith V. Jordan, et al. New York: Guilford Press, 1991.

Jordan, Judith V., Janet L. Surrey, and Alexandra G. Kaplan. "Women and Empathy: Implications for Psychological Development and Psychotherapy." In *Women's Growth in Connection: Writings from the Stone Center*, by Judith V. Jordan, et al. New York: Guilford Press, 1991.

Keen, Sam. *The Passionate Life: Stages of Loving*. San Francisco: Harper & Row, 1983.

Keller, Catherine. *From a Broken Web: Separation, Sexism, and Self*. Boston: Beacon Press, 1986.

———. "Toward a Postpatriarchal Postmodernity." In *Spirituality and Society: Postmodern Visions*. Edited by David Ray Griffin. Albany: State University of New York Press, 1988.

King, Ynestra. "The Ecology of Feminism and the Feminism of Ecology." In *Healing the Wounds: The Promise of Ecofeminism*. Edited by Judith Plant. Philadelphia: New Society Publishers, 1989.

Kingston, Maxine Hong. *The Woman Warrior: Memoirs of a Girlhood among Ghosts*. New York: Random House; Vintage Books, 1977.

Kwok Pui-lan. "Speaking from the Margins." *Journal of Feminist Studies in Religion* 8, no. 2 (Fall 1992): 102–5.

Loomer, Bernard. "S-I-Z-E." *Criterion* 13 (Spring 1974): 5–8.

———. "Two Conceptions of Power." *Process Studies* 6, no. 1 (Spring 1976): 5–32.

———. *Unfoldings: Conversations from the Sunday Morning Seminars of Bernard Loomer*. Berkeley, Calif.: First Unitarian Church of Berkeley, 1985.

Macy, Joanna. "Awakening to the Ecological Self." In *Healing the Wounds: The Promise of Ecofeminism*. Edited by Judith Plant. Philadelphia: New Society Publishers, 1989.

McDaniel, Jay B. *Earth, Sky, Gods & Mortals: Developing an Ecological Spirituality*. Mystic, Conn.: Twenty-Third Publications, 1990.

McFague, Sallie. *The Body of God: An Ecological Theology*. Minneapolis: Fortress Press, 1993.

———. *Metaphorical Theology: Models of God in Religious Language*. Philadelphia: Fortress Press, 1982.

———. *Models of God: Theology for an Ecological, Nuclear Age*. Philadelphia: Fortress Press, 1987.

Merchant, Carolyn. *The Death of Nature: Women, Ecology, and the Scientific Revolution*. San Francisco: Harper & Row, 1980.

Miller, Jean Baker. "The Development of Women's Sense of Self." In *Women's Growth in Connection: Writings from the Stone Center*, by Judith V. Jordan, et al. New York: Guilford Press, 1991.

———. *Toward a New Psychology of Women*. Boston: Beacon Press, 1976.

Morrison, Toni. *Sula*. New York: New American Library; Plume Book, 1973.

Ortner, Sherry B. "Is Female to Male as Nature Is to Culture?" In *Woman, Culture, and Society*. Edited by M. Z. Rosaldo and L. Lampere. Stanford: Stanford University Press, 1974.

Plant, Judith, ed. *Healing the Wounds: The Promise of Ecofeminism*. Philadelphia: New Society Publishers, 1989.

Plaskow, Judith. "Appropriation, Reciprocity, and Issues of Power." *Journal of Feminist Studies in Religion* 8, no. 2 (Fall 1992): 105–10.

Raymond, Janice G. "Female Friendship: Contra Chodorow and Dinnerstein." *Hypatia* 1, no. 2 (Fall 1986): 37–48.

———. *A Passion for Friends: Toward a Philosophy of Female Affection*. Boston: Beacon Press, 1986.

Ruether, Rosemary Radford. *Gaia and God: An Ecofeminist Theology of Earth Healing*. New York: HarperCollins; HarperSanFrancisco, 1992.

———. *Sexism and God-Talk: Toward a Feminist Theology*. Boston: Beacon Press, 1983.

Russell, Letty M. *The Future of Partnership*. Philadelphia: Westminster Press, 1979.

———. *Human Liberation in a Feminist Perspective—A Theology*. Philadelphia: Westminster Press, 1974.

Saiving, Valerie C. "Androgynous Life: A Feminist Appropriation of Process Thought" (The Harvard University Dudelian Lecture). In *Feminism and Process Thought: The Harvard Divinity School/Claremont Center for Process Studies Symposium*

Papers. Edited by Sheila Greeve Davaney. New York and Toronto: Edwin Mellen Press, 1981.

Schaef, Anne Wilson. *Women's Reality: An Emerging Female System in the White Male Society*. Minneapolis: Winston Press, 1981.

Shange, Ntozake. *Sassafrass, Cypress, and Indigo*. New York: St. Martin's Press, 1982.

Shiva, Vandana. "Development, Ecology, and Women." In *Healing the Wounds: The Promise of Ecofeminism*. Edited by Judith Plant. Philadelphia: New Society Publishers, 1989.

Soelle, Dorothee, with Shirley A. Cloyes. *To Work and to Love: A Theology of Creation*. Philadelphia: Fortress Press, 1984.

Spretnak, Charlene. *The Spiritual Dimension of Green Politics*. Santa Fe, N. Mex.: Bear & Company, 1986.

Starhawk. *Dreaming the Dark: Magic, Sex & Politics*. Boston: Beacon Press, 1982.

Stiver, Irene P. "The Meanings of 'Dependency' in Female-Male Relationships." In *Women's Growth in Connection: Writings from the Stone Center*, by Judith V. Jordan, et al. New York: Guilford Press, 1991.

Suchocki, Marjorie. "Openness and Mutuality in Process Thought and Feminist Action." In *Feminism and Process Thought: The Harvard Divinity School/Claremont Center for Process Studies Symposium Papers*. Edited by Sheila Greeve Davaney. New York and Toronto: Edwin Mellen Press, 1981.

Surrey, Janet L. "Relationship and Empowerment." In *Women's Growth in Connection: Writings from the Stone Center*, by Judith V. Jordan, et al. New York: Guilford Press, 1991.

———. "The 'Self-in Relation': A Theory of Women's Development." In *Women's Growth in Connection: Writings from the Stone Center*, by Judith V. Jordan, et al. New York: Guilford Press, 1991.

Swinburne, Richard. *The Existence of God*. Oxford: Clarendon Press, 1979.

Tan, Amy. *The Joy Luck Club*. New York: Ballantine Books; Ivy Books, 1989.

———. *The Kitchen God's Wife*. New York: Ballantine Books; Ivy Books, 1991.

Thistlethwaite, Susan. *Sex, Race, and God: Christian Feminism in Black and White*. New York: Crossroad, 1989.

Walker, Alice. *The Color Purple*. New York: Washington Square Press, 1982.

———. *In Search of Our Mothers' Gardens*. New York: Harcourt, Brace, Jovanovich, 1983.

Warren, Karen J. "The Power and Promise of Ecological Feminism." *Environmental Ethics* 12, no. 2 (Summer 1990): 125–46.

Washbourn, Penelope. "The Dynamics of Female Experience: Process Models and Human Values." In *Feminism and Process Thought: The Harvard Divinity School/ Claremont Center for Process Studies Symposium Papers*. Edited by Sheila Greeve Davaney. New York and Toronto: Edwin Mellen Press, 1981.

White, Lynn Jr. "The Historical Roots of Our Ecologic Crisis." *Science* 155 (10 March 1967): 1203–7.

Whitehead, Alfred North. *Adventures of Ideas*. New York: Free Press, 1967.

———. *Modes of Thought*. New York: Macmillan Company, 1938.

———. *Process and Reality: Corrected Edition*. Edited by David Ray Griffin and Donald W. Sherburne. New York: Free Press, 1978.

Williams, Daniel Day. *The Spirit and the Forms of Love*. Washington, D.C.: University Press of America, 1981.

Williams, Delores S. *Sisters in the Wilderness: The Challenge of Womanist God-Talk*. Maryknoll, N.Y.: Orbis Books, 1993.

INDEX

activism: and black feminism
(womanist thought), 20, 79, 109; and
consciousness raising, 21; and
ecology, 86; and friends, 3, 85; and
postmodernism, 130; and reflection
(praxis), 19; and separatism, 92; and
women, 84, 86, 87
actual entity (actual occasion, droplet
of experience, event), 20, 22, 23, 24,
25, 28, 52, 57, 59; experiencing
subject, 24, 52, 57, 94
Adair, Margo, 46
affective tone, 52
aggregates, 54–55
alienation: from body and matter, 45;
of humans from nature, 48, 50; of
male and female sexuality, 42; of
men from nature, 40, 41, 50; of men
from women, 40, 41, 44
Allen, Paula Gunn, 4, 39
animal: as living body, 50, 51, 53; as
person, 28; in relation to God, 122;
in relation to women, 39; as value,
55, 56
Anthony, Susan B., 77
Armstrong-Buck, Susan, 53
Asian feminist, 81–84, 103, 109
atomism, 43, 49

becoming, 23, 25
being: be-ing, 3, 69; being-in-
relationship, 2
Birch, Charles, 51, 55–56, 57, 58
black women: and black men, 5; and
white women, 4–5, 80, 96
body, 45, 50, 52, 54, 56, 103
Brock, Rita Nakashima: *agape* (as
unilateral power), 118; Christa/
Community, 30; erotic power, 30,
117–19, 122; God, 117; God/dess as
Heart (Heart of the Universe), 32,
118–19; patriarchal power, 117, 119;
patriarchy, 118; selfhood, 117

Carson, Rachel, 46–47
causal efficacy, 92–94
Chodorow, Nancy, 1–2
Christ, 125; Christa/Community, 30,
119
Chung Hyun Kyung, 82–84, 103, 109
class, 6, 7, 50, 78, 82, 83, 84, 85, 92,
95
coalition, 84, 86, 87, 93, 98
Cobb, John B. Jr.: coercive power,
112; creative love, 121, 125;
ecological model, 51; empowerment,
112; freedom, 30, 112; God, 29, 30;
gradations of value, 55–56, 57;
hierarchy, 51, 55, 56; Life as God,
58; lure for feeling, 58; lure of God
(call forward), 112, 120; nature, 51,
55; omnipotence, 111–12, 121;
person, 22; persuasive power, 30,
112, 121; responsive love, 123, 125;
rich experience, 56, 57
Collins, Patricia Hill: action and
thought, 20; black women's
organizations, 78; bloodmother, 79;
domination, 41, 43; either/or
dichotomous thinking, 41;
othermother, 79, 89, 122; sisterhood,
79; women-women relationships, 78,
79, 80
concrescence (emergence), 22, 23, 24,
25, 52
consciousness, 56
contrast, 57
control, 3, 26, 42, 43, 44, 46–47, 48,
114. *See also* power; omnipotence
cosmology, 13, 14. *See also* feminist
cosmology
creative process, 3, 25
creativity, 26, 91, 95; self-creativity,
28, 92, 93, 96, 116

Daly, Mary: Be-Friending, 3, 13, 68,
70–72, 85, 86, 87, 89; be-ing, 69,

135

in-fluence, 91; internal relations, 26,
91; patriarchy, 90; postmodernism,
32–33; praxis, 33; relational self, 26;
separate self, 26, 90–91; soluble self,
26, 90–91, 96–97
King, Ynestra, 4; body, 48; diversity,
48; domination, 47; ecofeminism,
47–48; hierarchy, 47; humans and
nature, 48; nature/culture dualism,
48; women and nature, 47, 48
Kingston, Maxine Hong, 4
Kwok Pui-lan, 81

language: castration, 101; gender
inclusive, 21; religious language,
108, 109
Lerner, Gerda, 93
lesbian: and female friendship, 71; and
feminist theology, 84; and gay
couples, 6; and separatism, 66
liberation, 82, 102, 119, 124, 125
living body, 50, 53, 54–55
living person (soul), 28, 51
Lobo, Astrid, 103
Loomer, Bernard: internal relations,
116; linear (unilateral) power, 30,
114; process-relational worldview,
30; relational power, 30, 114, 116;
relational self, 97; size, 97, 116;
unilateral love, 115
love, 3, 76, 106, 111, 112, 115, 118,
122, 125
lure of God, 25, 56, 58–59, 112, 120,
122, 125; lure for feeling, 58

Macy, Joanna, 4, 39
male-female relationship, 2, 5, 7, 41
matriarchy, 66
McFague, Sallie: experience and
reflection, 20; God, 9, 31–32, 105–6,
107; God as Friend, 106, 108, 109;
God as Lover, 32, 108, 109; God as
Mother, 106, 108, 109; immanence,
109; metaphors and models, 105,
109; nature, 106; organic model,
123; panentheism, 106, 109;
reformist and revolutionary feminists,
19; relational root-metaphor, 9;
transcendence, 109; world as God's
body, 32, 106, 109, 123
mechanistic worldview, 4, 14, 46;

machine economy, 33
Merchant, Carolyn: ecological
destruction, 40; mechanistic
worldview, 4, 40; nature as mother,
4, 40; nature as wild, uncontrollable
woman, 4, 40; Scientific Revolution,
4; woman and nature, 40
Mill, John Stuart, 16
Miller, Jean Baker, 2, 26
modern worldview, 32
Morrison, Toni, 5
mother-daughter relationship, 1, 2, 4, 6,
9, 67, 78
mothering, 1, 79
mujerista, 81, 83
mutuality, 3, 26, 29; with God, 31,
106, 116, 122; with nature, 39, 48,
125. *See also* reciprocity

naming, 65, 109
nature: alienation, 45, 47; "biophilic
bonding," 3–4; bodies, 48, 51;
continuity, 27, 50–53, 54, 60;
culture/nature dualism, 41, 43, 48,
60; diversity, 27, 48, 60, 61;
exploitation, 42, 125; friendship, 76;
God and nature, 27, 106, 122;
hierarchy, 47, 48, 49, 50;
independence and interdependence
with humans, 28, 37, 50;
interconnection, 27, 47, 50, 61;
pantheism, 104; power, 56; relations,
8, 10, 48; speciesism, 125;
subjectivity, 27, 56; value, 32, 55;
web, 47; women and nature, 4, 27,
28, 38, 39–41, 44–45, 48, 50. *See
also* animal
negative perception, 87–88
novelty, 58, 88, 89, 120, 122

object-relations theory, 1
omnipotence (divine power), 107, 108,
109, 110, 112, 120, 124; all-
controlling power, 110, 112, 121,
125; coercive power, 30, 112, 121,
124; empowerment, 109; erotic
power, 118–19, 122; hierarchical,
dominating power, 109, 124; love,
111, 121; patriarchal power, 117,
119, 124; persuasive power, 30, 106,
121, 124, 125; relational power, 121,